Book Selection and Censorship

A Study of
School and Public Libraries
in California

Book Selection and Censorship

By

Marjorie Fiske

UNIVERSITY OF CALIFORNIA PRESS
Berkeley and Los Angeles
1959

University of California Press
Berkeley and Los Angeles, California
Cambridge University Press
London, England

© 1959 by The Regents of the University of California
Library of Congress Catalog Card No. 59-10464
Printed in the United States of America

To the
Memory of my Father

HAROLD M. FISKE, SR.

This study was made possible by a grant from the Fund for the Republic and the sponsorship of the School of Librarianship of the University of California. During the period that the work was done (1956–1958), its director was a member of the faculty of the school. In the planning and analysis phases, Dean J. Periam Danton and Professors Fredric J. Mosher and LeRoy C. Merritt were invaluable in orienting the study staff to the profession of librarianship and the problems of censorship in California. Later they, Professor Anne E. Markley, and Professor Edward A. Wight contributed additional information and advice as the manuscript went through various drafts. Throughout the study Katherine G. Thayer, head of the Library School Library, provided significant information on materials and procedures in the field of librarianship.

The following persons served as members of the study's advisory committee:

David Blackwell, Professor of Statistics, University of California, Berkeley

Herbert Blumer, Professor of Sociology and Social Institutions, University of California, Berkeley

Jessie E. Boyd, Director of School Libraries, Oakland Public Schools, and Lecturer, School of Librarianship, University of California, Berkeley

Edwin Castagna, Librarian, Long Beach Public Library, (Chairman)

John Dale Henderson, Librarian, Los Angeles County Library

Harold Jones, Professor of Psychology, and Director, Institute of Human Development, University of California, Berkeley

Jerzy Neyman, Professor of Statistics, University of California, Berkeley

Nolan D. Pulliam, Superintendent of Schools, Stockton, California

Theodore L. Reller, Professor of Education, University of California, Berkeley

Carma Zimmerman, Librarian, California State Library

The members of the committee were most generous of their time in providing background information and suggestions which contributed greatly to the development of the study.

The executive boards of the California Library Association and the School Library Association of California offered the coöperation of their organizations, and the several regional and state meetings to which the study director was invited provided a perspective on library problems which would otherwise have been difficult to gain. Professors Seymour M. Lipset, Hanan Selvin, and Philip Selznick of the University of California, Berkeley, and Gertrude Jaeger Selznick offered helpful comments on the discussion draft of the manuscript. Above all, the substantive and editorial comments of my husband, Professor Leo Lowenthal, were major factors in the eventual organization of the report; and his sustained interest did much to relieve the usual isolation of writing and rewriting.

The field work of the study was conducted by Malcolm Roemer and Mary Viles. Their preliminary interviews and observations were invaluable in the development of the interview guides. Perhaps the most telling commentary on their creativity is that they were as productive and enthusiastic during the last phases of the field work as during the first. Interviewing, however, is a two-way undertaking, and the coöperativeness of the public and school librarians and the administrators who were interviewed was a continual source of gratification to the study staff. The frankness of their self-analyses, even when they believed they were incriminating themselves, testifies to the sincerity of their concern with the vital problems dealt with.

The key question was whether restrictions are being imposed on librarians, or whether they are imposing restrictions on themselves, that threaten the citizen's right to easy access to as adequate a collection of books and periodicals as his community, his county or his state can afford. Readers of this report may come to different conclusions about the "right" answer to this question, but whether they conclude that librarians are or are not being as forceful as they might be in developing and upholding freedom-to-read principles, it should not be forgotten that it is librarians themselves who have had the courage to provide the evidence.

After the completion of the field work, Mr. Roemer performed the tasks of quantitative analyst, qualitative analyst and editorial assistant. His ability to balance these three roles with no impairment of his quick perceptions and deep insights made it possible to employ more comprehensive analytical procedures than is usual for a study of this scope.

Ella Wolin served as secretary for the project, carrying out her varied and often burdensome duties with a combination of interest, precision, and responsibility that relieved the research staff of many harassments. The staff is most grateful to Annette Goodwin, Secretary of the School of Librarianship, for her guidance through the administrative channels and procedures of the University. We also wish to express our appreciation to Margaret Manson of the Central Stenographic Bureau for her expedition of the manuscript through various phases of reproduction.

Because of the coöperative nature of the study, the reader should be reminded that the deficiencies of the report are the sole responsibility of its author.

MARJORIE FISKE

Berkeley, California
March, 1958

Contents

I

Introduction

The impetus for this study developed from the questions librarians and others concerned with the freedom to read asked themselves about the effects on library policy and practices of the investigations of national and state un-American activities committees, state education committees, and the widely publicized book-centered conflicts which have taken place in California since the end of World War II. The study itself was viewed as controversial both inside and outside the profession of librarianship. Nearly two years of discussion and persistent effort on the part of the Intellectual Freedom Committee and a special planning committee of the California Library Association, as well as the faculty of the School of Librarianship of the University of California, were required before the decision to undertake it was finally made.

Selection of Communities

Twice, in the years between 1951 and 1957, library-centered community conflicts have occurred in California. Rumors of unpublicized episodes elsewhere were also numerous. It was at first intended, therefore, to focus the study on the ways in which librarians perceive and react to pressures exercised by individuals or groups within their own communities. In the planning stage, some thought was given to the possibility of conducting the field work in communities where different kinds of public pressures were known to have been exerted on school and public libraries and in a matched set of communities where no such pressures or episodes had been reported. Preliminary conferences with a number of public and school librarians in various parts of the state, however, soon made it clear that librarians' decision-making processes are strongly influenced by institutional pressures from within their own school or library systems, by public pressures outside their own communities, and by less specific but no less weighty pressures attributed to "the atmosphere of caution," or "the temper of the times." Furthermore, it became evident that many restrictive practices have been spontaneously incorporated into the routine procedures of both public and school libraries without any apparent external cause. It was decided, therefore, to study libraries in as wide a range of communities as time and funds would permit.

Twenty-six communities were selected on the basis of size, rate of growth, ethnic composition of the population, geographic location, and type of library service. The objective was to insure as wide a range of these variables as possible, in order to locate, define, and trace the interrelationships of the significant factors involved in the selection and distribution of controversial materials under varying circumstances. The field work consisted of 204 interviews with school librarians and administrators, and municipal and county librarians in forty-six senior high schools, and forty-eight municipal and county units in twenty-six communities. (Characteristics of the communities selected and of the individuals interviewed will be found in Appendix A, tables 1–7.)

In a strict statistical sense, the findings of this study cannot be projected to the communities, institutions, or librarians in the state as a whole. But since the institutions and respondents included in the sample are responsible for library service to a majority of the state's population, the picture would probably remain the same if the study were repeated with a true cross section.

FIELD WORK

In each community the head librarian of the municipal library, the head of the county library system (if one was situated in the community), the superintendent of schools or such persons as he might delegate, senior high school principals, and school librarians were interviewed. Within each public library, interviews were conducted with as many staff members responsible for book selection or for book selection policy as time allowed. In the largest cities, where complete coverage of library branches or of senior high schools was not feasible, an effort was made to cover as wide a variety of districts (in terms of socioeconomic factors) as possible.

Before the interviewers went into the field, school superintendents and head librarians received letters describing the study, its purposes and its sponsorship. An article about the study's objectives and procedures appeared in the journal of the California Library Association,

California Librarian, well before the field work began. The 204 interviews were conducted with about equal proportions of county librarians, municipal librarians, school librarians, and school administrators. In addition, there were some seventy-five preliminary conferences and interviews. Two-thirds of these were exploratory, and formed the basis for preparing the first draft of the interview guide. The remaining third were pretest interviews undertaken in order to refine the guides and to train the interviewers. These interviews have not been coded or tabulated, but some material gathered in them, especially information about major book-centered conflicts, has been included in the report.

The objective of the early conferences and interviews was to determine which factors loom largest in the minds of librarians and school administrators as they think about book selection and controversial material. From these preliminary explorations, a list of topics was developed that includes the factors most relevant in book selection, again with particular, but by no means exclusive, emphasis on the perception and handling of the controversial. (By this time it had become apparent that a number of seemingly irrelevant factors were significant by default.) This list of topics was included in an interview guide which was then revised several times in the course of the pretest interviews (final versions of the interview guides will be found in the appendices). At the same time, attention was paid to the development of follow-up and probe questions most likely to elicit full responses. Several data sheets were drawn up to record factual material about the community, the institutions, and the individuals included in the study.

Throughout the regular field work an effort was made to retain the flexibility which characterized the preliminary interviews. The subject of the study was introduced in very general terms and the respondent was encouraged to speak at length on all factors most relevant to him. Then the interviewer continued with questions pertaining to topics not spontaneously mentioned by the respondent. The interviewers first introduced a topic with direct, open-ended questions of a general nature ("How about community organizations, do you ever think about them when you are selecting books or thinking about book selection policy?"). Only when the respondent did not reply with concrete data or opinions of his own volition did the interviewer ask specific questions ("Could you tell me which groups? Have they ever raised any objections?"). To provide confirming material and to encourage discussion by respondents who did not "open up" in response to general questions, a number of additional "probe" questions were introduced. For example, having asked general questions about the respondent's attitude toward controversial books, the interviewer might later ask what the respondent would do or had done with *Peyton Place* (if he had not mentioned it spontaneously). Or, having discussed how the librarian felt in general about the attempts of groups or individuals to super-impose their views upon library practices, the interviewer might then inquire if the librarian had encountered any such attempts within the last few years and how they were handled. (It had become clear during the preliminary interviews that general opinions are not necessarily consistent with action or even with attitudes toward concrete situations.)

Notes were taken in the course of an interview (except in the rare exceptions where respondents objected), and insofar as possible the interview was written up in detail immediately after its completion. In most instances, the interview was reconstructed in the sequence in which it occurred; and where such information was relevant, the interviewer noted which topics he had introduced and which were introduced spontaneously by the respondent. The interviewer also described the general setting of the interview, the respondents' manifestations of interest or disinterest, and his own reaction to the respondent where this was conceivably a significant factor. The interviews ranged in length from half an hour to six hours, the average being slightly under two. The short interviews, for the most part, were with school administrators. Some were too busy for a longer session; others showed little interest in the subject and made haste to turn the interviewer over to the librarian. Transcripts of the interviews totalled about 1,500 single-spaced typewritten pages.

By and large, the respondents were coöperative and showed great interest in the study. In only some half dozen cases was there clear evidence of antagonism toward the interview, the interviewer, or any particular topic. There were occasional objections to some kinds of background information requested or to the request for opinions on what were interpreted as irrelevant issues; but they were rare and in themselves constituted significant data for the study.

Except for two cities where the interviewers divided the interviewing between them, a single interviewer went to each community. With few exceptions no more than three communities were covered without a return to headquarters for at least a week of review and discussion.

ANALYSIS

The analysis proceeded on three levels: coding and tabulation, "horizontal" analysis (all relevant topics, all interviews), and a series of "vertical" analyses of each interview, individually and by various groupings.

The code covers factual information about the communities, the institutions and the respondents, and a number of attitude and behavior categories. After coding, these data were transferred to McBee cards. Because of the smallness of the sample, and because we were interested in the interrelationships of various factors rather than with projectible figures as to their frequency, the tables were limited to straight counts and simple cross-tabulations. Only those cross-tabulations have been drawn on which show distinct reversals or gross differences, or when the change in the relationship between two variables has been both consistent and marked in a single direction.

The horizontal analysis began with a listing of topics encompassing the bulk of the material in the interview transcripts. After checking and regrouping, this list was reduced to some one hundred categories (see appendices). Each paragraph of each interview was then coded in accordance with this topical list (most paragraphs had multiple codes), cut, and pasted onto a card. It was thus possible to draw decks containing all material relevant to a given topic. These decks were subjected to both quantitative (where numbers warranted such an approach) and qualitative analysis.

This description of analytical procedures does not reflect a time sequence. Actually, the main themes and subdivisions of the report were tentatively determined before tables were run and before the card decks were analyzed. The basis for the development of this detailed outline was the vertical analysis, or rather a series of analyses, of all interviews. They were first read by institutions within each community; they were then re-grouped and analyzed in various categories such as professional function of the respondent, professional training, city size, and the like. With each grouping, themes were elaborated and hypotheses developed.

Further groupings and re-readings of the interviews determined which tables should be run and which decks should have priority in the horizontal analyses. In effect, the vertical analysis amounted to a series of condensations of all interviews from different thematic standpoints and in a variety of sub-groupings, such as school principals in comparison with librarians in their own schools. Throughout the analysis these re-readings of the interviews in different groupings and from different viewpoints produced insights which were then checked against tables and card decks. It might be added, for those who are interested in the techniques and validity of the analysis of qualitative materials, that practically all of the many hypotheses and speculations which arose in the course of the impressionistic vertical analyses proved valid when checked quantitatively or by systematic study of the card decks.

The six remaining chapters of this report fall into three subdivisions describing the general setting (chaps. 2 and 3), the encounter with and the treatment of the controversial (chaps. 4, 5, and 6), and some general implications for professional organizations and institutions (chap. 7).

2

Book Selection
Theory and Practice

The basic function of librarians—to bring people and books together—is deceptive in its apparent simplicity. If we conjure up a library Garden of Eden with a librarian who has had the best available training, has overcome all personal prejudices, is supported by a capable board, and is unhampered by financial stringencies, we still should find a far from idyllic situation. Librarians must interpret and anticipate the needs of a vast, uncoördinated and unpredictable assortment of human beings. They must evaluate and select the material to meet these needs from an overwhelming mass of publications that include numerous items about which no two people are likely to agree. The librarian, in short, is the matchmaker in a continual marriage of diversity and disparity.[1]

Dimensions in Book Selection Doctrine

The philosophies of librarianship reported by participants in this study vary from summary statements about getting people and books together to complex expositions about the library as a "dynamic repository of

---

[1] No major study of the book selection philosophies and practices prevalent in public and school libraries has yet been undertaken. We can only scratch the surface of this complex here, attempting to provide some indication of the scope of these philosophies and practices and, in particular, of their relationship to prevailing attitudes and behavior in regard to controversial materials. Discussions of book selection philosophies and problems are found in a member of the more recent standard works of the profession, such as: Sidney H. Ditzion, *Arsenals of a Democratic Culture* (Chicago: American Library Association, 1947); Robert D. Leigh, *The Public Library in the United States* (New York: Columbia University Press, 1950); Helen E. Haines, *Living with Books; The Art of Book Selection* (2d ed.; New York: Columbia University Press, 1950); Lucile F. Fargo, *The Library in the School* (4th ed.; Chicago: American Library Association, 1947); Louis R. Wilson, ed., *The Practice of Book Selection* (Chicago: University of Chicago Press, 1940). There is

humanistic values." There is no single dimension that will accommodate all of these approaches; they consist, even for a single person, of inter-locking long- and short-range components, ideological and operational, abstract and concrete. "Quality" and "demand," two rather general and time-honored values, can be construed as the extremes of a con-tinuum on which most librarians may be found; but they are likely to hold other concepts which conflict with their attitudes toward these two values.

The writings of Western scholars, theologians, literary critics—even booksellers—beginning at least with those of the Elizabethan era, have been threaded with observations about quality versus demand in read-ing materials, or as they more often expressed it, about education versus entertainment. By the eighteenth century, especially in England, where literary products became wares in the market place and broad seg-ments of the population began to buy them, scarcely a writer of note failed to explore the matter in some detail. At first, the crusade for uplift—moral, spiritual, and educational—was paramount. But as maga-zines, inexpensive books, and lending libraries flooded the market and bookselling became a major business, a conflict developed. Writers and philosophers began to see the ends of literary endeavor—education and entertainment—as mutually exclusive. By the middle of the eighteenth century spokesmen such as Samuel Johnson were attempting to recon-cile these two ends with the argument that the educational and up-lifting must also be entertaining or it will not be effective.

Throughout these early debates there was a special concern for youth. If you give young people adventure, romance, or horror stories, argued Defoe and Goldsmith, not only may their values and their morals be corrupted, but the time spent in pursuit of such passive pleasures will be stolen from more important social pursuits such as economic or in-tellectual betterment.[2]

The themes of this early controversy were continued in the speeches and writings of American librarians throughout the nineteenth and early twentieth centuries. After World War I a new note was sounded. The basis of education was being broadened: every American child should go at least through secondary school; standards, intellectual, literary or moral, it was felt, could no longer be handed down by tradi-

---

little agreement among these authors, however, on the long-range goals of public and school libraries, or even on the history of library philosophy.

[2] For further discussion of the debate at this time, see "The Controversy over Art and Popular Culture in Eighteenth Century England," by Leo Lowenthal and Marjorie Fiske, in Mirra Komarovsky, ed., *Common Frontiers of the Social Sciences* (Glencoe, Ill.: The Free Press, 1957).

tion, or imposed authoritatively by an elite, to be assimilated only by the few capable of rising to them. Instead, standards should be adapted to the disparate capacities of the population and, since pedagogic potentialities also varied and were further limited by depletion of energy and the number of hours in a day, the adjustment of standards was inevitably, according to this reasoning, downward.

What was the consequence of this change for librarians? They did not abdicate as educators, but they did become more aware of the pluralistic nature of their clientele; they paid attention to different "reading levels" and they developed a greater tolerance of what they might formerly have rejected as "mere trash." If popular literature attracts people to the library, they reasoned, perhaps it can become a steppingstone to something better. Since the librarian could not read every book and periodical being published, it was perhaps a happy circumstance that he could justify the "pure entertainment" sections of his collection on grounds that they might lure the reader on to more serious efforts.

With the advent of economic depression, this justification was no longer necessary. Americans too poor to pay for their customary amusements sought out the library for the first time. It was easy for the librarian to believe that any means could be justified if they provided these new patrons some relief from harsh reality. In short, what librarians sometimes refer to as a "social service" concept of librarianship came to outweigh, and in some neighborhoods even to supplant, the concept of the library as an institution devoted mainly to the development of intellect and sensibility. Although book purchase funds were sharply curtailed in the depression years, most collections reflected the greater responsiveness of librarians to the entertainment side of the equation. Those several librarians who can look back upon this period, seem to have found considerable relief in being able to resolve or at least reduce the tensions of the old dilemma by responding to the pressure of social and economic events. The high demand for escapist material persisted through World War II. Tensions, anxiety and stress remained sharp realities of life and the library, reasoned the librarian, not only had a right but an obligation to provide relief.

Today, we once more find signs of conflict. Librarians live in a milieu which is highly self-conscious about the importance of democratic procedure and increasingly uncertain about the role of the professional. Like the school principal who was shocked by a parent's advice to a son who was not getting his own way in high school—"remember that principals are just employees"—the librarian is sometimes taken aback by the taxpayer who considers his own judgment of books as good as the professional librarian's. In addition, a few persons from every walk of life feel that it is their duty to keep watch on what other people are reading. Such persons, it has often been observed, rarely read—least of all the materials they deem subversive or immoral.

Self-appointed censors, however, have doubtless existed since writing was invented. More recent, and more serious, is a generalized anxiety conveyed to librarians by serious and tolerant citizens from whom they would normally expect solid support for the library and its traditions. What the librarian sees are prosperous communities where every child will get at least a high school education and a majority of children will move on to college or a well-paying job, and the many amenities of modern life. But he senses anxieties and tensions as powerful as those of the depression and war years.

A generation ago, active interest in public educational institutions was limited to a relatively small group of citizens. Most of them were college-educated or rather well self-educated people of middle age with higher than average social and economic status. Typically they were acknowledged and accepted by their fellow citizens as "the folks who keep an eye on everything that goes on here in town." To be sure, most librarians can still point to a handful of key figures in their communities. But they notice a change: the influential people now derive their authority from—and therefore are beholden to—broader and more mobile segments of the population than they did two decades ago. "Everything is so unstable these days . . . people move around so much, there's not even a traditional-type nucleus of community-oriented families in many towns any more."

What are the reasons for this change? It is possible that greater concern with human relations and social problems in secondary schools and in colleges has strengthened the sense of civic responsibility among a higher proportion of the population (half of the adults in California are high school graduates, and a college degree is increasingly commonplace). In depression periods, the interest of the civic minded focuses on social services; in wartime, on various aspects of civil defense. In a period of prosperity and comparative peace, public educational institutions are crucial enough and expensive enough to attract attention—the more so in a state where the rate of expansion of such facilities is so great that bond issues and higher taxes for plant development and personnel recruitment are continually in the public eye.

In the past, there were few doubts about the virtue and viability of the American tradition, and perhaps for that reason there was more tolerance for specific studies and discussions of ideologies of the extreme left and of the extreme right than is the case today. The American way of life, put to the test of depression and war, seemed to emerge triumphant. Now there are no clear-cut tests, only a sense of danger and threat. Perhaps, this logic continues, the responsible citizens of today should keep watch on the people who run the schools, who teach, or who manage the libraries. Thus far we have managed to avoid Communism and atomic warfare. We do not know how we avoided them, and, not knowing, one way to maintain our safety is to let nothing change. Educators and librarians deal with ideas; and they may be more liberal than most. They must not be allowed unwittingly to become victimized by their own good intentions and naïveté, because they are in charge of idea-transmitting institutions.

When a patron enters the library he may make it very clear that he is not interested in—that he wants to avoid—serious thought about the enigmas of our time. "There isn't a *problem* in this book, is there?" is a question some librarians said they hear with increasing frequency. This climate is not interpreted by librarians to mean that the citizenry is inclined to take ideological action but they believe the public is more alert, more concerned, more aware of those who do take action. A school superintendent who participated in the study summed up the irony of this situation by saying that it is at once a tribute to Americans' faith in the power of ideas and an avoidance, possibly through fear, of their substance. A head librarian's summary was more pessimistic: "Everything the library stands for," she said, "runs counter to the prevailing trends of our time."

Two-thirds of the public librarians [3] who contributed to this study used the words quality and demand as they discussed library objectives, and by far the greatest weight was to be found on the side of demand. Among the sixty-nine public librarians who described their philosophies of librarianship in these terms, thirty-eight believe that the library's chief function is to meet public requests; five are primarily value-oriented, and the rest hold mixed or contradictory views.

The demand-oriented librarian often justifies his policy on the grounds that the public library is supported by the taxpayers' money: "When you are operating with tax monies, you have to meet the public's tastes with little regard to trying to raise those tastes." [4] Some-

---

[3] Throughout the text, "public librarians" refers to municipal and county librarians unless otherwise noted. The word "librarians," unless qualified, includes school as well as public librarians.

[4] The quotations used throughout this report have, unless otherwise noted, been selected as representative of the viewpoint under discussion.

times this view is rationalized as the result of a tacit or explicit division of labor: "It is not the librarian's job to educate; that is the function of the school." A corollary to the demand approach is the consideration of what the taxpayer does not want, or what he believes is inappropriate for a library collection. As might be expected, most librarians with restrictive attitudes toward controversial materials are to be found on the demand side of the continuum.

The size of the geographical areas that the county library systems of the state must serve seem to have made it necessary for most of them to cater to public demand at the expense of building basic collections.[5] Nevertheless, the proportion of adherents to the demand philosophy is no greater among county librarians than among their municipal colleagues. Both county and municipal librarians occasionally added a cautionary phrase or two to their demand viewpoints, suggesting that public wants should be tempered by professional judiciousness. The head of a municipal library for whom "Two things are necessary to any business, to have the goods and to be accommodating. The librarian is here to serve the public, to give them anything they want . . ." added that the librarian should of course use "good judgment" in the choice of books. The order librarian of a county system who rather pessimistically observed, "Most of the time one book is as good as another, so you may as well buy the one they're asking for," also said, "I constantly compromise with what I believe." What she believes is that the library should concentrate on "worthwhile" reading matter. She is not alone among county librarians with personal inclinations toward building a quality collection, but most of them believe that as public servants they have no right to "impose" their views. The one county system in the sample which is notably quality-oriented pays, according to its order librarian, a penalty. "We take the traditions of humanism, of personal growth, into account even if it means a slight circulation. But maybe that's why we have budget trouble; we can't back up our arguments with the Board of Supervisors." Another county librarian observed that meeting the reference needs of patrons is more important in the long run than circulation, but added that the sheer size of her county and its scattered population makes it practically impossible to provide such resources.

The conflict between circulation volume and value to the community is clearly revealed in respondents' praise of the resources of the Cali-

---

[5] County service units, except in the largest systems, are circulation outlets only, and the great majority have a major turnover in their collections within six months to a year. Reference resources are almost non-existent at most county branches covered in this study; such resources are maintained at the central library and are available to branches and service units on request.

fornia State Library. Rare, foreign, or highly specialized books borrowed from this collection for local patrons comprise only a fraction of 1 per cent of any local unit's circulation; yet the value of such material is widely praised by county and municipal librarians alike. "How could you run a library without access to those materials?" asked the head of a middle-sized institution who, almost in the same breath, had endorsed the popular demand viewpoint.

The demand approach eases the tasks of the librarian in a number of ways. Certainly when appropriations depend on circulation figures (as is the case in most branches, and many entire systems) the quantity-minded executive has less difficulty in justifying a budget than does the quality-oriented librarian. "Our job is to get the borrower of a book together with what he wants . . . there's no alternative, really, because no one will take what he doesn't want, and then circulation would go down." Another demand-oriented municipal librarian explained that a major rationale of her approach, particularly when the clientele wants "westerns and more westerns," is economy for the taxpayer: "We save an awful lot of people a lot of money by buying this stuff for them." (In sharp opposition to this policy, another municipal library recently all but stopped the purchase of mysteries and westerns. As one of its staff members explained, "it was sinful to spend all that money on that stuff," and he went on to say that no drop in circulation has yet been noted.) Such time-consuming problems as allocations by subject matter and the development of a basic or well-rounded collection become largely irrelevant if you are "dedicated to patron demand," as the head of a municipal library in a large (close to 100,000) industrial community explained. Book selection becomes "a snap"—the desk staff pass along patron requests, you read the newspapers of the area, visit the bookshops to find out what is popular, and if you miss something a patron wants you can always dash out and buy it.

Twenty-six of sixty-nine public librarians who talked about library objectives in terms of quality and demand seemed at first to be demand-oriented. In the course of their interviews, however, they introduced values which suggest that they endeavor to hold the two concepts in equilibrium. About one-half of this group emphasized the importance of distinguishing between demands and needs. "Demands," as a representative of this view remarked, "are merely what people want; needs are what exist as a result of their condition of life." The other half expressed apparently unequivocal allegiance to a demand philosophy, but described specific library objectives and practices in terms which were clearly value-oriented. They spoke of their interest in promoting education, personal enlightenment, and taste. When asked to relate these two seemingly inconsistent ideas, they pointed out that cultural improvement can be achieved only by keeping people reading, that book selection geared to public demand is justified chiefly as a means of keeping people within the librarian's sphere of influence. This was the "come-on" approach succinctly summarized by the head of a library in a small town: "You give the community what it wants and at the same time dangle something better in front of it." This combination of views is more likely to be sustained by librarians in small and medium-sized communities who emphasize that such an equilibrium can be maintained only if the staff has personal contact with a high proportion of patrons.

The five public librarians who stressed value at the expense of demand were persons with strong faith in the individual's capacity for development. "Readers," one remarked, "are more discerning than they are given credit for." These librarians feel sufficiently secure as professionals and as members of the community to have no qualms about spending money for the person with out-of-the-way or above-average interests. "If only one person reads the new collection of Mannheim's essays in a year, it is more important than if one hundred read the whole bestseller list."

These quality-dedicated librarians share with many of the twenty-six who endeavor to hold the concepts of quality and demand in equilibrium certain characteristics which identify them as "marginal." Most of them had professional training and experience in other fields before entering library work, or their careers in public librarianship were not typical. Some, for example, had worked in universities, in adult education, or in public relations. They are aware of "bucking the tide," or they feel an implicit antipathy between public library traditions and the standards of contemporary life. They harbor a sense of crusade which is stronger than among other respondents, and they are the severest self-critics and critics of what to them is opportunism and superficiality in the professional organizations and training schools. Quality-oriented school librarians show these characteristics even more strongly.

We shall discuss the school librarian's philosophy in a later chapter. Suffice it to say now that they place great importance on the quality of their collections. When a school librarian speaks of "demand," she refers to teacher requests and "curriculum needs," not to the wishes or interests of readers. The equivalent of the value-demand continuum for the school librarian is the range between "the development of a love of reading" and "supplementation of the curriculum." Like the public librarian who wholeheartedly espouses the demand theory, the school librarian who stresses curriculum supplementation tends to be cautious in book selection and restrictive in the circulation of controversial materials.

The two other concepts most frequently used in discussing theories of librarianship were on very different levels. One, the idea of *balance*, was used in reference to the operation of a library; the other, the concept of *moral commitment*, focused on the librarian's motivation.

Library schools have used the word "balance" most frequently to describe a well-rounded collection. Prescriptions for building basic collections for public or school libraries illustrate this concept by recommending definite proportions for various categories of subject matter with little regard for community differences. In practice, particularly in the smaller public libraries, the contours of a collection seem to develop informally. In the words of the head of the circulation department in a city system, "Balance just happens." The term itself, however, continues to carry a kind of professional sanction for public librarians (as does "to supplement the curriculum" for the school librarian). It was used in the interviews as if it conveyed a self-evident truth: "Of course you want a balanced collection, and you always bear that in mind when you are selecting books." But on further questioning it turned out to be a semantic convenience embracing a great variety of rationales for book selection.

Many librarians simply used the word to describe the goals of whatever aspects of book selection they find most trying. The head of a small city library, who inherited an archaic, crowded collection, thinks of balance as something to be achieved mainly by discarding old books. For those preoccupied with problems of community relations or controversiality, balance may mean "covering many points of view" or "all sides of a question." Some demand-oriented persons defined balance as the establishment of an equilibrium in meeting the wishes of a variety of patrons: "Balance in a collection can come only from balancing the needs of the persons served," or, "Balance implies buying for the minority as well as for the majority." Librarians who sensed a conflict between the two goals of building a collection of permanent value and meeting public demand said that balance is "a dynamic equilibrium between a sound collection and demand." If they favored the demand side, balance was viewed as a relationship between actual and potential wishes of the patrons: "You try to maintain a balance between expressed wants and what they would want if you helped to lead them to it."

Some librarians feel that the use of the term balance is outmoded. This was suggested by a county branch supervisor who feels that the cultural-educational function of the public library is a thing of the past. She used the word balance frequently, but finally brought herself up short: "We talk a lot about balance, but it is really a semantic absurdity. What it boils down to is that you provide as much as you can of what anybody wants." [6]

Nearly all librarians, in discussing their philosophies of librarianship, made some reference to ideals, inspiration, or dedication. About 15 per cent of them believe that a strong moral commitment is the *sine qua non* of librarianship. "You don't make much money as a librarian —at least I haven't—but it is a rich and varied and wonderful life. . . . The human capacity for development is infinite, and librarianship provides an incomparable opportunity for your own fulfillment and for helping others." They pointed out that an inspired idealism is the best defense against censorship pressures. Persons holding such views are usually able to avoid reacting defensively to the particulars of an attack on the library by justifying its long-range cultural objectives. There is more evidence of this inspirational attitude among school than among public librarians, and it may be closely related to their stronger feelings of isolation. They believe the sense of dedication sets them apart from run-of-the-mill teachers and administrators; and the isolation, in turn, reinforces their moral commitment.

THE SELECTION PROCESS

Since meeting public demand is seen as a major library objective, we might expect that the gauging of community needs would be a major preoccupation. But this proved not to be true. Respondents discussed the process of evaluating the supply at great length; references to gauging needs, either of patrons or of the community at large, were brief. The evaluation of supply was often described as an elaborate, systematic, and sometimes scientific process. The gauging of needs was intuitive. "You keep a kind of file in your mind. You read a review and think about your public and how the book would fit for them." This "playing by ear" book selection procedure is used in most municipal libraries having only one or two professionals on the staff. In larger institutions, there may be group discussions or group decisions, or an

---

[6] For additional semantic problems encountered by the profession, see chap. 4 "Semantic Conveniences," pp. 60–63.

order or head librarian may analyze and collate the suggestions of many staff members. But even when several staff members participate, and when special aspects of community needs are evaluated, the underlying process remains essentially the same. You "think about your public" as you "read a review."

Gauging needs.—Regardless of their position on the quality-demand continuum, all public librarians believe that the "needs and interests of the community" require consideration; but on the question of how to assess these needs there is little agreement. Librarians in the largest systems pass over the problem lightly. As one observed, if you buy nearly half of all books published each year, you can't help but supply most of what is wanted or needed; if some desires remain unsatisfied, there is enough money left to cover them too. Librarians in towns of 7,500 population or less, and many of those in the next size class (up to 25,000), feel that their first-hand acquaintance with individuals and groups in their communities enables them to guage needs almost automatically. In the communities of medium size (25,000 to 100,000), librarians who are most demand-oriented believe that the review of patron requests—those made in writing or those reported by the desk staff—constitute an adequate assessment of community requirements.

County librarians and municipal librarians in the middle-range cities who are not wholeheartedly demand-oriented express the most dissatisfaction with their methods of gauging community needs. County librarians responsible for book selection rely mainly on reports of patron requests relayed to them by personnel in the branches; occasionally someone from the headquarters staff goes into the field to assess turnover in various categories—but few are satisfied with such appraisals. Heads of municipal libraries stress the importance of participation in community groups, and a number of them take desk duty now and then as means of getting acquainted with patrons and "feeling out" trends. Persons from these middle-range libraries were most likely to point out that one of the greatest needs of the profession today is for a practicable method for assessing public interest or need. "We really have no idea what the actual or potential interest is. I wish we could do some research," complained the head of a county system. Another county librarian remarked, "The schools do surveys to assess needs all the time, but requests are our only survey." [7]

We might expect that book-buying decisions would be made in the light of what is now at hand either in the institution's own collection

---

[7] Both the California State Library and the American Library Association have sponsored workshops on how to assess community needs, but neither organization has funds at its disposal to assist local libraries in making such surveys.

or in other libraries accessible to its patrons. Actually, such considerations are pretty much ignored. Very few of the librarians studied have any information which could provide them with an up-to-date picture of how their collections are distributed among various subject matter categories. Nearly all public and school librarians know how much money was spent for books in their institutions in the past fiscal year and about how many volumes (but not necessarily how many titles) were purchased. Most, but by no means all, know approximately how many books are in their collections (though some head librarians reported that estimates sent annually to the State Library might be off as much as 10 per cent). Head librarians and children's librarians know the proportions spent for adult and children's collections, and some cite rough allocations among non-fiction, fiction, and reference materials. But aside from the general acknowledgment of deficiencies in technical material, few public librarians spoke of their collections in terms of narrower subdivisions such as history, biography, or social science.

Systematic allocations play a small role in making decisions about new purchases. The public librarian's attitude is epitomized by the one who said, "There is little point in establishing categories or allocations for new purchases because you have to be flexible; public interest is not predictable." School librarians may say: "We do not purchase by subject category allocations because we are curriculum oriented, and we never know when the curriculum may shift." Or they point out that interest in the library differs greatly from one teacher to another, and with the current high turnover in most school faculties such planning would be impracticable.

Inventories have not been undertaken on a regular basis in most institutions studied, a fact which makes the task of becoming acquainted with a collection a rather staggering one for new staff members. Lack of specific information about a collection also affects the processes of discard and replacement which to many librarians is as important a discriminatory function as that of selecting new books. A few public librarians have, on occasion, tried to make spot appraisals of their collections in order to determine gaps in various subject fields as a guide to future buying. The most systematic of these efforts have been made by order librarians in larger county systems. The municipal librarians in medium-sized communities who have made such attempts soon gave them up for want of time or money.

Despite complaints about the unpredictability of the curriculum and of faculty indifference toward the library, school librarians are more concerned with over-all appraisals of their collections. About half of them try periodically to fill out each subject area with "basic" material, whereas only one-fifth of the public librarians reported taking subject categories into account in the process of selection. This greater attention to the collection as a whole, to inventorying and to systematic weeding out, is more urgent and at the same time is more manageable in the schools. Even in a large high school the number of volumes is fewer than in a small town public library, and there is more dependence on material considered to have "permanent" value, for which guidance is available in selection sources. County library systems, with their inevitable shifting about of books from branch to branch, suffer the greatest insufficiencies in collection evaluation.

Evaluating the supply.—Evaluation procedures described by respondents relate almost exclusively to the selection of newly published materials. To be sure, librarians are occasionally faced with the necessity of building up a basic collection or overhauling an old one, but this task is rarely viewed as overwhelming, because the handbooks of the profession offer both guiding principles and specific recommendations for libraries of various sizes.

The selection of new materials was acknowledged as one of the primary functions of the professional, but librarians agreed almost unanimously that they do not have enough time for it. The only exceptions were a few subject specialists who spend all of their time in evaluation, and head librarians in the largest institutions who delegate book selection to their staffs. For the rest, estimates of the time spent in book selection ranged from one-tenth to one-third (rare) of the work week.[8] Except for children's books, few materials acquired for the public library are read in advance by a staff member. In all sizes and types of libraries, it is the book review which forms the basis for the librarian's evaluation of current supply.

The review sources which librarians consult as a basis for becoming acquainted with the new books and for evaluating them may be divided roughly into professional sources (ALA *Booklist*, special compilations of the American Library Association, *Library Journal*,[9] the various Wilson

---

[8] Fargo, *op. cit.*, cites a 1941 U. S. Office of Education report on a sample of eleven high school libraries whose librarians spent an average of 5.9 per cent of their working time on all phases of "book acquisition" while giving more than 40 per cent to non-professional tasks "at least some of which apparently might have been turned over to others." Our findings suggest that "working time" considered in this breakdown obviously excludes evening homework or week ends in the office, when perhaps a major portion of book selection for school and small public libraries is done.

[9] This journal is not sponsored by any professional association but it is published and written by professionals and is widely viewed by librarians as a "professional" source. Wilson publications are similarly viewed.

Catalogs), trade or commercial sources (such as the Kirkus Service and *Retail Bookseller*), and general sources including local newspapers, *The New York Times Book Review*, the *Saturday Review*, and a number of monthly journals. Altogether some two-dozen printed standard sources were mentioned.[10]

Public and school libraries in the largest and smallest communities use more sources than do those in the middle range. An average of 12.7 general sources are used in public libraries in cities of 100,000 or more and 7.6 in communities of less than 25,000. Only 5.6 are used in communities falling in the 50,000 to 100,000 category. Differences are less striking for school libraries, yet the trend is parallel: those in communities of between 25,000 and 100,000 have recourse to the fewest sources. The head of a municipal library in a medium-sized community who remarked, "We are institutionally adolescent," may have provided a clue to this seeming deviance of the institutions in the middle range (a deviance which was also apparent in respect to gauging community needs and appraising present collections). Such libraries are expected to fulfill most of the functions of their counterparts in the larger cities, yet their staffing patterns and their budgets resemble those in small towns. They are rarely departmentalized, have few specialists, and are often run by persons without professional training who "grew up" in the system. Similarly school librarians from communities in the middle range report the least time for book selection and the greatest amount for clerical or non-library functions. In contrast, the large public and school systems are highly departmentalized, have many operational and subject matter specialists, and a sufficient budget to buy the tools they require.

The high dependence on reviews in the smallest communities is due in part to the paucity of colleagues with whom information and ideas can be exchanged. Some of the small towns in our sample are so isolated that there can be little interchange with neighboring professionals. And, while all libraries have fiscal limitations, a ten dollar purchase requires more careful evaluation in a book budget of one thousand dollars per year than it would in one ten or twenty times that size.

---

[10] No attempt was made to compile a complete list of all sources used at each institution; rather, we encouraged respondents to discuss those which were used most frequently and considered most useful or reliable. Altogether, there were 356 "mentions" of such sources, but intra-institutional repeats were deleted, leaving 286 references for the thirty-five systems. The average number of regularly used sources reported from the thirty-five public libraries or library systems was 8.2 per institution. In the thirty-five schools from which data were collected on this topic, an average of 4.3 sources per school was reported.

Public and school librarians differ considerably in their use of reviews: professional sources account for 63 per cent of those regularly drawn upon by school librarians, as compared with 41 per cent of those used in public libraries. Conversely, trade journals, publishers' catalogs and other commercial periodicals account for less than 1 per cent of the sources used in schools, but for 17 per cent of those used in public libraries. Literary weeklies and monthlies such as *Saturday Review, Harper's The Atlantic* and *The New Yorker*, and the leading newspaper book review sections are about equally popular in school and public libraries.[11]

The most important sources for public libraries are, in descending order of frequency of use: *Kirkus' Service* (25 institutions), *Library Journal* (23), *The New York Times Book Review* (23), one or more of the Wilson Company's publications (22),[12] *Saturday Review* (21), and the ALA *Booklist* (20). Among schools, Wilson publications and ALA *Booklist* rank first (28 and 24 institutions, respectively), with *Saturday Review* (19) and *Library Journal* (17) coming next. Kirkus is used only by one school librarian interviewed, and she does not subscribe to it but occasionally browses through issues at the public library. The school librarian, generally more concerned with the content of books and with their impact on readers, turns for assistance to those sources which provide the most specific information. The public librarian, generally more attentive to demand and less committed to educational objectives, turns more to sources which have broad coverage and are timely. School librarians also pay more attention to "basic lists" in order to review subject matter areas for purposes of filling in or maintaining balance in their collections. Wilson materials, the American Library Association's *A Basic Book Collection for High Schools* and special topical lists were mentioned as particularly useful by more than half the school librarians. In discussing how and why the various tools are used, school librarians were also more specific than their public colleagues.

Public librarians are likely to have an ambivalent attitude toward their book review sources. There were more spontaneous comments about the service of Virginia Kirkus than about any other tool, and they ranged from great appreciation to great annoyance. Small town librarians are the most grateful for this service. Some of them rely upon it almost exclusively not only for information about what is available

---

[11] A summary table of the sources drawn upon by school and public librarians will be found in Appendix A, table 8.

[12] Including, variously, the *Bulletin* and the *Children's Catalog, Standard Catalog for High School Libraries, Fiction Catalog,* and *Standard Catalog for Public Libraries,* and their supplements.

but for advice on whether to purchase. "The Kirkus reviews are helpful," said one such librarian, "because they are written from a librarian's point of view . . . whereas the others review the books in a vacuum." Furthermore, the Kirkus reviewers know, or purport to know, what is likely to be offensive to small town library patrons. In the words of a county librarian: "Sometimes she says 'not for public library.' That's a flag to watch." Or, more specifically, "One thing a librarian always has to keep an eye open for is the sex problem. I don't think any of us want our libraries to get the reputation of having improper books. . . . If Virginia [Kirkus] says it's obscene, that decides it . . ."

Frequently the warnings are read with misgivings, particularly in larger systems: "It's nice the way Kirkus warns if there's a question of suitability. . . . But sometimes she does annoy me. . . . It's funny how part of me appreciates her warnings and at the same time another part of me resents them." Reservations about the Kirkus service are particularly strong among librarians who have had professional training. To accept the service's evaluation as tantamount to a purchase decision is in their opinion, a waiver of professional responsibilities. "There are reviewers who mark a review with a 'recommended for a public library.' This is ridiculous. Nobody can select for *this* library except the librarian . . . in this community." Or again, "I don't know if you can depend on Kirkus. . . . There's something so pat about her reviews. The tone is not of discussing and offering helpful information, but of making up the librarian's mind for her. That just doesn't appeal to me." The one positive attribute willingly conceded to this service is its timeliness (many publishers provide the firm with pre-publication proofs); that, these critical librarians believe, is the only possible excuse for using it. Conversely, the criticism most frequently applied to other sources which are considered more reliable is that they appear too late to be useful to the public librarian.

Another frequent complaint about many sources, professional as well as commercial, was that the qualifications of the reviewers are not specified, and criteria of relevance and standards are not stated. *Horn Book*, a review digest of children's books, is evidently an exception. It provides reviewers' backgrounds and has spelled out its criteria of relevance so consistently over the years that children's librarians allot it the same confidence they would a trusted colleague.

Librarians who have time to read the reviews exhaustively believe that if enough sources are used over a long period of time, special biases are no longer a problem because they can be recognized and discounted. But most librarians do not have time to steep themselves so thoroughly in the sources. This is one reason why review sessions of groups of librarians from one large institution or from several smaller ones are increasingly popular. Books reviewed at these sessions are previously read by the reviewer and briefly summarized at meetings, in the course of which recommendations to purchase or not to purchase are made. If there is any disagreement in the group, the chairman may bring the matter to a vote, but decisions more frequently are informal. In the words of one enthusiast, these sessions are

. . . invaluable . . . There's no substitute for reading a book . . . because guidance is so important in working with children. . . . A few minutes of oral presentation can present infinitely more than an extensive written review can. Even the professional reviews convey remarkably little which is useful for guidance work. Of course, seeing the book . . . is best, but considering the impossibility of this the review sessions are a wonderful substitute.

Sources other than printed or oral reviews are occasionally mentioned by public, rarely by school, librarians. Book club choices are automatically purchased in nine institutions (including some for the children's sections), and in three there is some reliance on the advice of dealer or bookstore personnel. Nine spoke of visits of publishers' representatives, but opinion varied as to their helpfulness; three find them "very reliable," while the rest believe they are considerably less so than they used to be. The same was said of the publishing houses themselves. There was a time when much selection was made on the basis of the publisher's reputation for specialization and reliability. These matters were and still are discussed in book selection courses. But several of our respondents observed that such information quickly becomes outdated, and the standards and selection patterns of publishing houses are not so predictable as they were ten or twenty years ago. Today, librarians may avoid a given publisher on some such grounds as "dripping sentimentality" or "propaganda," but rarely will they favor one on grounds of general reputation. Publisher reliability is considered somewhat more consistent for children's books.

Children's material is exceptional in another respect. Only when our respondents spoke of literature for children did they discuss at length, or with any degree of specificity, the standards they apply as they read reviews or the books themselves. School and public librarians alike seemed to agree that reading level, adequacy of print, paper and illustrations, "developmental level," and, in fiction, "imaginative level" (or "esthetic validity") comprise criteria which can be applied with some degree of unanimity to children's literature. The most specific comments about the selection of material for children (and they are uniquely specific) came from a high school librarian.

Well, for example, say you're considering whether to buy Henry Miller or Steinbeck. . . . Now, Henry Miller, I don't see that there's anything to it that has any constructive value in a school library. . . . But Steinbeck, that's got literary value, eloquent prose, good character development and a social message. What more can you want in a novel?

Underlying this agreement about standards for children's literature is the belief that adults read book reviews and bestseller lists. They know what they want; children do not. Children, therefore, can and should be guided "away from trash" and shown "alternatives and values." "There is enough good material [for children] so that it is inexcusable to buy bad. Whatever the demand is, there is always something qualitatively acceptable." Reinforcing this point of view are two other concepts. One is that since children do not pay taxes, the library is not obligated to meet their expressed wishes. The other is related to the psychology of reading. About one-half of the public librarians and a third of the school librarians touched upon the latter subject. They pointed out that librarianship has "special responsibilities" to children, and that these responsibilities become most complex and critical when applied to adolescents. One-half of the school librarians who discussed this topic—as compared with one-fifth of the public librarians—believe that books can have a harmful, even traumatic effect on readers not sufficiently mature to cope with certain aspects of life (references were mainly to sex and to political propaganda). "You wouldn't try to teach Einstein's relativity before they've had algebra," in the words of one, or, "You don't race a colt before he's saddled and shoed."

Few public librarians believe there is any real need for "protecting" children from books. Most are frank to say that their "special responsibility" is designed not to protect children or young people but to protect themselves from parents. Quite a number went out of their way to state their belief that books do not harm people, that the child who is too immature for a book will not understand it and probably will not even read it. A few pointed out that we really know nothing about the impact of books, and, until we do, "If you're going to slap their hands every time you're not *certain* they won't get hurt, you might as well close up the library."

Making the decision.—Questions about the ultimate responsibility for evaluation and selection were answered on two levels: in terms of legal authority and in terms of actual practice.

In county systems, the final responsibility for book selection is clearly vested in the head librarian. In municipal systems the legal situation is more ambiguous. Authority is usually vested in the board of trustees and it may or may not be formally delegated to the head librarian.

Municipal librarians' authorities and responsibilities are, typically, the cumulative product of many years of board rulings recorded in unindexed minutes, or not recorded at all. The new librarian is especially hard put to know what rulings may or may not have been established before his employment. The county librarian's authority is explicitly stated in "An Act To Provide for the Establishment and Maintenance of County Free Libraries," *California Statutes.* (This provision was subsequently incorporated in the *California Education Code.*) A number of county as well as municipal librarians, however, did not have a clear idea of the limits of their legal responsibility. But they did not consider the matter particularly important. In the minds of most librarians in all types of institutions there is no doubt that only the professional library staff should have *de facto* responsibility for book selection. Close to 80 per cent of both school and public librarians hold this view. Among those who do not concur with the majority, are public librarians who believe that "public requests" should be the ultimate criterion or that the board of trustees or county board of supervisors should have the final say.

The legal situation is fairly clear-cut in the schools. All books are purchased over the principal's signature, even in districts where the book selection process is centralized in the office of the superintendent. The principal's authority is delegated from school board and superintendent, and the principal, in turn, delegates final decisions to the librarian. He signs the order list, but only in rare instances does he review it in any detail. This is a practice which most school librarians consider appropriate. Book selection, they point out, is the business of the professional librarian. Either the principal has confidence in her decisions or he replaces her. In our sample of schools only when the school board had actively participated in book selection, or when the principal or superintendent was uneasy about public pressures, did school administrators play an active role in the selection process. We shall see later, however, that this does not mean that they have no influence on this process. The few school librarians who do not believe that the professional librarian has ultimate responsibility defer to principals or teachers in making book selection decisions. Among those school librarians who believe that responsibility should be vested in the librarian, half feel that in the event of a flare-up over controversial materials their own authority should be superseded by that of faculty, administration, or supervisory personnel in the office of the superintendent.

In practice, the decision-making process in book selection may be roughly summarized as follows: In small town libraries and in the

smallest county systems, which normally have only one or two professionals, the entire process is the head librarian's responsibility. It may
be shared with another professional, if there is one, or (occasionally)
with one or more board members. In institutions of medium size (three
to nine professionals) the dilemmas of "adolescence" appear, and a
variety of arrangements have developed. All members of the staff
normally make suggestions, but final decision-making may be entirely up to the head librarian or may depend on staff consensus. In
the large institutions (ten or more professionals) all professionals make
recommendations, but the bulk of the suggestions and all evaluations
are likely to be left to a small committee or to the order librarian.

The role of the heads of county and municipal branches in book
selection is undefined.[13] In the huge county systems and in two large
municipal systems, the branch heads, even those with professional
training, do not participate in book selection. They merely forward
patron requests and make their own selections from a centrally prepared list. Many branch heads, particularly those with professional
training, regret this lack of participation in the selection process, and
their discontent is sometimes increased by what they believe to be an
arbitrary handling of their requests at headquarters. To facilitate participation by branch heads, one large county system recently decen-
tralized its book selection procedures by assigning regional supervisors
to coördinate sub-groups of branch libraries.

Professionals in county, municipal, and school systems in the middle
population range, on the other hand, spoke much of the need for
centralization of the book selection process. In most cases, centralization is thought of as an adjustment to growth, "to assure every student,"
as one school librarian said, "of equal opportunity in the library." But
it is frequently looked upon as a protective device as well. Those who
favor it tend to be cautious in their own book selection policies and
the least outspoken on freedom-to-read issues. Those who strongly
oppose it are more likely to resist restrictive pressures.

When there is doubt about the circulation of a book, when it is
known to be controversial, or when it is thought to be potentially
controversial, reading the reviews does not always suffice—the book itself may be read. An order librarian in a county system, for example,
reported that she herself reads a book if, on the basis of disagreement
among reviewers, it appears to be "too good" (i.e., will not circulate)

---

[13] "Branches," as used in this report, refers to any circulation outlet subordinated
to a headquarters unit; nine of the seventeen branches visited were headed by librarians with professional schooling (degree or certificate, usually in addition to a
B.A. degree).

or "too bad" (i.e., risqué or politically dubious) to purchase. She also reads books about which branch heads have reported unfavorable comments from patrons. Another county order librarian reads, or asks some other staff member to read, all material on which the review sources disagree, and all "otherwise controversial" material. Such first-hand screening, however, is a luxury feasible only in the larger systems. The head librarian of a smaller county system or of a municipal system in a city of fewer than 100,000, and the school librarian who makes decisions on her own, are quite likely to solve the screening problem by not buying anything about which any doubt has arisen.

3

THE CONTEXT

At best, book selection is a process of compromise. It is also the aspect of librarianship in which the prerogatives of the profession are most subject to interference. Book budgets are slashed arbitrarily; personnel problems are indifferently "solved" by civil service boards whose regulations barely distinguish between the techniques of book cataloguing and those required for the filing of street repair supply invoices. Officially, all librarians must reckon, directly or indirectly, with the judgments—or caprices—of board members. Unofficially, most librarians are also constantly aware of the support, obstructionism or indifference of those voluntary associations which represent, or purport to represent, organized public opinion in their communities.

This chapter describes how the people who make selection decisions view these broader contexts within which their professional tasks are carried out. School administrators, school librarians, municipal librarians, and county librarians all agree that library boards, school boards, and county boards of supervisors as well as voluntary organizations help to create the atmosphere of which they are aware as they make their book selection decisions, but they are by no means in agreement when it comes to estimating the degree of this influence.

THE COMMUNITY AT LARGE

School superintendents and principals, though highly conscious of the views of their boards, are almost equally sensitive to the special interests of the more prominent voluntary organizations in their communities. Principals in metropolitan systems where supervisors or curriculum coördinators plan and direct school library policy from the superintendent's office, however, proved to be notable exceptions to this rule. When they mentioned the school board or voluntary organizations as factors to be taken into account in the operation of the library they did so only in passing. Their references to "headquarters" or "central" were also casual, often self-consciously so, as though the respondent wished to convey the impression that the book selection functions performed there are essentially a "service" to the individual schools. But further probing made it clear that the casual tone was a face-saving device. Autonomy in book selection does not, in fact, exist in metropolitan high schools; but with lack of autonomy comes increase in protection. All of these metropolitan principals assume that if community pressures were directed against their particular libraries the matter would be dealt with in the office of the superintendent.

With a similarly perfunctory bow in the direction of autonomy, school librarians in these larger systems report that they are "of course" responsible to their principals. But in their discussions of book selection problems and procedures references to "downtown" predominate, and sooner or later in the interview most of them confessed that they feel like mere distribution lackeys. Whatever mention they made of school boards or community organizations were paraphrased quotations of someone in the headquarters office.

Librarians in medium-sized and smaller systems rarely expressed opinions of their own about school boards or community organizations. Community relations, these librarians believe (or, in some cases, are told), is the province of their school's administrators.

Heads of county library systems are also comparatively unconcerned with the agencies of the city or town in which they work. The headquarters of a county system does not customarily provide library service to the community in which it is located, the county seat usually having its own municipal library. The public, to the head of a county system, is the county at large, exclusive of those pockets in it which are served by municipal libraries.[1]

The county supervisors are an immediate but not an infringing reality for the county librarian, primarily because such bodies are normally so busy with roads, health, and numerous other responsibilities they are glad to delegate all library functions except the required annual review and approval of the budget.

Librarians who run county branches, for their part, pay more attention to the central library than to the agencies of the communities they serve. As in the large municipal systems, books are selected at

---

[1] The historical basis of this situation is discussed in Leigh, *The Public Library in the United States.*

headquarters, with only nominal contributions from branch personnel. Furthermore, the county branch library is less a community institution than the municipal library, because its official channels to and from the public are through the office of the head county librarian. The librarians in charge of county branches are not unaware of the structure and elements of the cities and towns in which they work. They may be active participants in community affairs, but the impact of such participation is indirect. To influence policy it must be relayed to headquarters and taken into account there.

The hierarchy of influences that heads of municipal libraries describe resembles that of the school administrator. In metropolitan systems, headquarters filters and deflects the impact of the branch head's experience of the community he serves. In middle-range and small cities and towns the librarian is very conscious of the power structure of the community and of the importance of good public relations with organized groups and the press. The city librarians and the school administrators differ, however, in their views of their respective boards. For the principal or school superintendent, the school board (elected) [2] is ever present in considerations of policy and sometimes in considerations of practice. Among the chief executives of municipal libraries, the role of trustees (appointed) [3] is by no means as predictable. In some cases the board is drawn into book selection matters at the librarian's initiative, in others the board takes initiative, and in a few it plays no role whatever. In communities where there is a city manager, the head librarian may circumvent the library board altogether. Among staff members in municipal libraries, children's librarians are the most community conscious, possibly because in many units they head a library within a library and are semi-autonomous. Branch heads in municipal systems do not differ greatly from their counterparts in county systems. The few who participate in the central book selection process are most likely to be aware of and interested in the function of the board of trustees and the role of voluntary associations.

Awareness of boards and of voluntary organzations, in short, fluctuates in accordance with the complexity of the bureaucratic structure in which the individual works and his position in the hierarchy. It is keenest among school administrators and heads of municipal libraries who run independent institutions. For those in large systems, head-

---

[2] In three California cities, Alameda, Sacramento and San Francisco, the school board is appointed. All other California school boards are elected.

[3] Two cities in our sample have no library board. Where boards exist, however, they are appointed. (The State also has seven library districts, embracing small communities and their environs, which have elected boards. Such districts constitute a negligible fraction of the State public library scene; none of them were included in this study.)

quarters is the more immediate reality. Staff members, whether they are school librarians or members of county or municipal library systems, tend to reflect their superiors' attitudes. Local newspapers and other media were singularly ignored in our respondents' discussions of the broader environment in which they work. As we shall see, however, they influence book selection both indirectly and by default, and, in communities where library controversies have occurred, local newspapers have played decisive roles in their outcome.

BOARDS AND TRUSTEES

The role of the school board in library policy.—Of all board and professional relationships, the one between school administrator and school board is the most clear-cut: principals and superintendents agree that their boards should formulate policy or at least participate in its formulation; several believe that boards have "a right to intervene" at any level of the school system. Such intervention may be resented, but rarely does the administrator question either its existence or its prerogatives. On the contrary, the local board is often highly valued as protector of the school administration from those real or threatened encroachments from "the state" which haunt the local superintendent or principal with a special persistence.

In comparison with this concern of the school administrator about the possibility of state intervention, his relationship with the local school board is relatively placid. Nevertheless, nearly all superintendents and principals who spoke at any length of their boards confessed to a fitful concern with the problem of where the administrator's authority ends and that of his board begins.[4] Even those who believe that the school board has the vested right not only to formulate policy, but to interpret and enforce its implementation at all levels of the school system, pointed with some irritation to situations where the exercise of this "right" has obstructed the machinery or interfered with the goals of the educational system. They criticized boards which have taken the initiative in banning specific books or authors from school libraries, for example, not because these were censorial actions but because they introduced confusion and uncertainty into the system and lessened the autonomy of the professional staff. On the other hand, a school board that periodically sends a committee into school libraries to check on whether books were being used enough to warrant the investment of taxpayers' money, while considered a nuisance, was not accused of exceeding its proper functions.

---

[4] *Boardsmanship; A Guide for the School Board Member* (Stanford, California: Stanford University Press, 1955) discusses these problems in a practical framework.

Very few school administrators, however, had any first-hand grounds for complaints about board interference with library policy or practice. The major exception was a conflict over UNESCO materials in Los Angeles in 1952, and this was not a matter in which the school board made the first move. The incumbent board was attacked by persons and organizations in the community at large. The board which succeeded it in the next election acted on the assumption that its mandate from the people was to reverse the policies which had been under attack—particularly those pertaining to the treatment of international relations in the schools. This board did indeed "reach down" and veto certain library books as well as other teaching materials. (See chap. 4, for further details of this controversy.)

For the rest, school boards have occasionally initiated discussions of book selection policy or, more often, have participated in policy discussions at the suggestion of the administration. Only one board, aside from that in Los Angeles, was reported to have proscribed a book on its authority alone. It banned Lincoln Steffens' *Autobiography* not from the library but from a "recommended reading" list. Three school boards have reviewed and endorsed written statements of school library book selection policy at the request of the principal or superintendent. Three more took a stand on particular controversial books, in two instances because the administrator or the librarian wished to be assured in advance of board support in the event of public objections, and in one instance simply because the administrator believes his board should be involved in practical problems from time to time.

Despite their *pro forma* acceptance of unlimited board rights, few administrators consider it advisable for the board to act directly either in book selection policy formation or in controversies about books. Their attitudes on the subject became particularly clear when they discussed library-centered episodes that have taken place in other parts of the state. In one community, where a school board publicly confronted a would-be book burner, the conflict turned into a victory for freedom of the library. But a number of administrators felt that the superintendent could, and should, have handled the matter himself, avoiding both board involvement and open conflict by behind-the-scenes discussions with the complainant, or by quietly replacing the controversial books with "more up-to-date ones." These were administrators who believe that school boards should never be invited to discuss library matters because "entangling" the board in this fashion is tantamount to "asking for trouble." School librarians, on the other hand, do not always see eye-to-eye with their administrators. They voice the opinion that open discussions, even if they turn into conflicts, clear the air by clarifying the function of the school library and the respective responsibilities of board, superintendent, principal, faculty, and librarian.

On the few occasions when school administrators went out of their way to praise their boards, it was to emphasize the members' understanding of the responsibilities of the professional. These were invariably in communities where school boards had been elected with little regard to politics, whose members were eminent and respected leaders of the community who relied upon the superintendent to bring to their attention matters requiring their advice or decisions. However widespread the acknowledgments of the pervasive rights of a board, this kind of delegation seems to be regarded not only as the traditional relationship between board and staff, but as the ideal one.

Municipal library boards.—Unlike school boards, most municipal library boards in California are appointed by the mayor or the city council. Appointment to a library board is often regarded as a minor political plum, but no librarian in this study reported evidence of partisan bias among board members. The prototype of the library trustee, according to the descriptions offered by our respondents, is an active or retired business man of late middle age. In metropolitan areas various religious and ethnic groups common in the community are represented on the board, along with an occasional university or college administrator or professor. Among library trustees it is not unusual to find spokesmen or unofficial supporters for groups which are restrictive or censorial in matters relating to public education.

As might be expected, library boards pay more attention to book policy or to particular books than do school boards which must cope with many matters in addition to libraries. Even so, in only five of the municipal libraries covered in the study is there evidence that the board has initiated discussion or action in this direction. Two boards were in small towns where the members make a practice of helping the librarian by suggesting new acquisitions. A third board, after hearing of a book controversy in another part of the state, voted to have a written book selection policy formulated. The fourth board, in a community having a vigorous anti-education press and some voluntary organizations markedly restrictive in their approach to education, has tried, with little success, to impose prohibitions on the library. At the time of the field work for this study, a member of that board was campaigning to have books labeled as to the "political bias" of the author. The librarian opposed this proposal and thus far no labeling has been undertaken. She attributes her successful resistance largely to the fact that, with the appointment a few years ago of a city manager, she, as the head of a city department, acquired a double set of superiors. If the board does not support her policies, she can turn to the manager. In the matter of labeling, the manager endorsed her stand. Moreover, since the remaining trustees were not unequivocally committed to the proposal, their energies, again with the encouragement of the city manager, were easily redirected toward bond issues and plans for a new library building. Members of the fifth board which has frequently taken a stand on book policy and on particular books are evidently content simply to express their points of view. Their directives have become buried in hundreds of pages of minutes, and no one on the library staff has the time to forage for them. This same board once set up a subcommittee to evaluate books, but dissolved it later on the grounds that "none of us knows anything about books."

The board of trustees of another municipal library regularly reviews lists of all prospective purchases for the library, a procedure suggested by the city manager. The librarian responsible to this board reported that it initiates the only restrictive pressures exercised on the library. Its most recent objection, which originated with a Roman Catholic member, was to Kinsey's works. On this occasion the board's directive not to purchase the books was overruled by the same city manager who suggested that it review all purchases in the first place.

This is a second example of a disagreement between librarian and board settled by the librarian's appeal to the city manager. Similar circumventions were found in county systems where the librarian reports both to county administrative officers and to boards of supervisors. In general, county and municipal librarians welcome the opportunity for recourse to civic administrators. Some of them, not surprisingly, report that their trustees or boards view city and county managers as a threat. City managers have "executive authority" while the trustees of the library have "legislative authority," and there is sufficient ambiguity in each of these authorities to allow an enterprising librarian considerable leeway. In the instances reported by our respondents, the city manager does seem to have the right to overrule the board in library policy and practice. This *de facto* power seems to derive from his function of reviewing and coördinating department budgets before their submission to the council. In communities having no city manager, the mayor or city council presumably has similar authority, but no examples were reported in which trustees questioned or resented it. The explanation may be that library trustees expect to be responsible to the elected official who appoints them, but not to another appointee.

As with school boards, when trustees of a municipal library take an active part in book selection policy or become concerned about particular books, it is usually at the initiative of the librarian. If, for example, a book controversy in another community leads a librarian to conclude that a written policy is in order, he may present the idea for board discussion and later may submit the policy for formal approval. Only one municipal librarian reported taking the attitudes of board members into account in routine book selection. This was in a small town where "nothing risqué is bought because the board might curb me," and where it seemed clear that the attitudes of the board were not threatening to the librarian's sense of professional autonomy because they closely resemble her own.

Municipal librarians were more critical of their boards than were school administrators, but their complaints were less specific. Board indifference rather than board interference is what rankles, and it was most often attributed to perpetual incumbency or to the use of the post as a reward for minor political services. Actually, the greater frequency with which librarians complained about their boards may not mean that they are more dissatisfied than the school administrators are with theirs, but may simply reflect a greater willingness to criticize an appointed than an elected body. Library trustees do not come up for re-election; they have no "platform" and no "mandate." They therefore are sometimes looked upon as less representative of the public interest than an elected body. But no librarian ventured to suggest that library boards should be elected—on the contrary, even librarians who most strongly believe that the library's function is to meet public demand do not favor such a possibility. A few are convinced that the system of trusteeship is obsolete, and point out that direct responsibility to the city manager, council or mayor, like that of any other municipal department head, would be a more efficient chain of command for the librarian.

The librarian's relationship to his board is clearly influenced by his status in the community. Librarians who have circumvented their board's attempts to impose restrictive measures by an appeal to the city manager or mayor are typically persons of some stature in the community for reasons independent of their professional standing. On the other hand, when the board consists of persons of eminence and the librarian is a newcomer or has little prestige in the community, the librarian is likely to go to great lengths to solicit board support. Librarians whose status is about on a par with the board rarely attempt to circumvent it, nor do they go out of their way to obtain assurance of board support. A similar connection between community status and relationship with boards may be detected among staff members of municipal libraries. In general, only head librarians showed any marked interest in the function or activities of the trustees. The exceptions are children's librarians, whose relatively independent status in the library has already been noted, and a few assistant librarians whose community status is at least as high as that of the head librarian.

The county supervisors.—More often than school administrators or municipal librarians, county librarians were certain that their boards of supervisors would support their book selection policy and any consequences of it that might develop in the event of controversy. Only one example of a county board suppressing books, an ancient and long since removed ban on John Steinbeck's *Grapes of Wrath*, was reported in the study. Remembering this, however, the county librarian, after the suppression of Edmund Wilson's *Hecate County* in another part of the country, felt it advisable to tell her board that the library had several copies of the book. After this consultation a number of board members decided to review the book personally. According to the librarian, no firm decision was ever made about it. The books were never returned to the collection, however, and she assumes that they are still circulating among board members' friends.

Like the heads of municipal libraries, many county librarians remarked that their boards are indifferent, but this observation was seldom made in a complaining tone. The county librarian is not as exposed to public pressures and he therefore has less need for a buffer. His sphere of authority is more clearly defined. Board indifference allows him wide latitude in which to fulfill professional obligations without incurring anxiety. Like other librarians, the head of a county system may regret the lack of official enthusiasm for his libraries, but he is usually a very practical and efficient administrator himself and can readily and undefensively attribute the supervisors' lack of interest to the fact that they are heavily burdened with other aspects of county administration.

VOLUNTARY ORGANIZATIONS

The attitudes of our respondents toward voluntary organizations ranged from painful and continual awareness of the pressures they exert or might exert to occasional uneasiness about their indifference to the library. No school administrator or head librarian singled out an organization as supportive of the values for which the library stands, but nearly all of them expressed the hope that improved public relations would eventually change the situation. The more pessimistic attitudes prevail in communities where extremist groups are known or thought to be active; the more energetic public relations efforts are being made in communities where less predictable groups (notably the American Legion) have in the past conducted campaigns against books or authors. School administrators and heads of public libraries tend to have similar views of local organizations.

In one large city, however, there was no such agreement. Two or three local organizations had waged vigorous and highly publicized "pro-American" campaigns, and the reports on their activities offered by school and county library respondents were very similar. They named groups and their leaders. They described their efforts to suppress certain ideas, books, and authors, and several expressed the hope that the present study might help to buttress school and library resistance to such pressures. Respondents in the city system, however, many of whom had the impression (presumably conveyed by their superiors) that the study's main focus was on organized pressure groups, did not mention these organizations at all. The majority went out of their way to point out that "we have been lucky," without specifying the nature of their good fortune, but strongly suggesting a desire to avoid a discussion of external pressures. Despite extensive publicity about restrictive campaigns waged by extremist groups against county and school libraries, all respondents in this system pointed out that only the head librarian could be expected to have an opinion on such matters.

Similar avoidance was noted in another large city where the school library system is firmly controlled by the office of the superintendent and where the public library's relations with organized groups are limited to contacts of the head librarian and one or two others on the headquarters staff. School librarians said that opinions about community groups were definitely not their business. Public librarians reported that they had been told to avoid contact with all organizations. Again the interviewers felt that, with few exceptions, the respondents were going out of their way to avoid mentioning any group by name. One school librarian did report some pressure from a local PTA, but it was exerted so long ago that she could not remember when. (The PTA had complained about Gayley's *Classic Myths* because of "incest among the gods." The book was removed from the school system and has, to the librarian's knowledge, never been returned.)

One-third of the references to voluntary associations were to groups generally considered to have "extremist" programs (such as Freedom Clubs and Pro-America). These organizations, sometimes identified by name and sometimes referred to more vaguely as "fringe groups," were mentioned as actual or potential sources of pressure against both school and public libraries. All references to locally active extremist organizations were found in six of the twenty-six communities, five of them clustering in the southern part of the state.

Among the organizations identified as having neither uniform nor

consistent programs, restrictive or otherwise, veterans' groups pre-
dominated. The American Legion was referred to more often than any
other veterans' organization, more often, in fact, than any group of any
kind; but most of these references were in the past tense. Respondents
remarked a noticeable decline in the interest of the Legion in published
works following its pressures for the removal of "un-American" materials soon after the war. (As of November, 1957 the national policy
of the Legion against teaching about communism in the schools was
reversed.)

The Legion's concern with textbooks, however, penetrated well into
the consciousness of public as well as school librarians. A number of
school administrators have joined their local Legion posts and have
maintained close informal relationships with the frank objective of
forestalling future attacks, an objective which they believe can be obtained by convincing members that "the local schools are their schools."
A few head librarians and school administrators make a point of informal "clearance" with the Legion when they initiate a new program
or policy which seems within the group's interest, or when they suspect
that "trouble" may be brewing.

Civic organizations.—Civic organizations are generally described as
supporting plant expansion but being indifferent to the less "tangible"
issues of intellectual freedom. In a few communities where there has
been public controversy over school texts or library books, one or more
civic organizations (PTA's, Women's Clubs, The American Association
of University Women, The League of Women Voters, and similar
groups) have played an active role in maintaining free procedures or
policies.[6] Their activities, however, do not seem to be generally known
in other communities. Even if they were it is unlikely that librarians
would feel encouraged, because, as they frequently point out, there is
little uniformity of program or behavior among the local units of such
national organizations.

PTA's were mentioned more than any other civic group. This organization is a source of considerable distress to school librarians because
of its apparent indifference to school library problems, whether of a
controversial nature or not. One school librarian who had formerly
worked in another part of the country observed that California PTA's
are more conservative than those elsewhere, that they are not inclined
to take sides in a controversy or to take a stand on an issue. A perusal

---

[6] The role of organized groups in community controversies over school library
or public library holdings is being analyzed in a series of case histories by Zane
Meckler of the Community Relations Council, Los Angeles, and Professor Richard
Morris of the University of California, Los Angeles, under a grant from the Fund
for the Republic.

of reports of the three major school controversies which have taken place in the state since the war (Pasadena, Los Angeles and Marin County) suggests that PTA's did not play as decisive roles in the outcome as did some other civic groups. It should be recalled, however, that only senior high school librarians were reporting. The picture might be different on the junior high or elementary school levels. In some communities PTA's have been active in establishing library collections where none existed, and in putting pressure on school board or administration for establishing the post of school librarian.

While school librarians regret the lack of PTA interest in high school libraries (one did report, with some pride, a recent invitation to speak on the function of the school library before a local unit), a number of public libraries reported that local PTA's had formed or were forming nuclei for the establishment of Friends of the Library groups.

Business associations.—Business associations were less frequently mentioned than civic organizations, probably because there are fewer groups which fall into this category than under the more general rubric "civic." When such organizations were mentioned at all, however, they were viewed as potentially more powerful than those whose interests are mainly civic. School administrators and public librarians assume that their local chambers of commerce and taxpayers' associations will, as a matter of principle, fight every proposal which involves an increase in taxes. A few librarians and school administrators invite representatives of business organizations to attend board meetings where potentially controversial subjects are introduced. Others clear new plans with them, informally, and as a matter of course. These practices are more common among school administrators than among library executives. They are one more manifestation of the coöperation between business and education exemplified by the practice (an annual event in many California cities) of declaring a city-wide school holiday during which the students are set free while the faculty visit local business, industrial and commercial plants.

Religious groups.—Religious groups are mentioned most often in smaller communities; in communities under 7,500 they were sometimes the only types of organized groups discussed. One public librarian in a small town, after observing that "this patriotism business has gotten pretty extreme these days, and probably especially in California" went on to note that, "up here the sort of person who might tend toward fanaticism becomes a church stalwart and lets off steam that way." Most complaints based on religious convictions usually bear on questions of morality and are made by people who identify themselves as members of a specific denomination but do not claim to represent or speak for the group. Unlike the allegations emanating from the American Legion or the Veterans of Foreign Wars, which are sporadic, reproaches from religious groups are perennial. Library or school administrators are rarely exposed to particularly vehement charges from such sources. When they are, the usual recourse is to seek the coöperation of the clergy. In one case a woman purporting to represent a church group entered the school library with a list of "treacherous" books. The school administrator telephoned the woman's minister, who assured him that, while she belonged to his congregation, she did not represent a church group and that he personally would take care of the matter.

Some religious organizations shower the library with gift materials. The customary procedure is to accept all or some of it, providing that comparable reading matter from all major religious groups in the community is available. Catholics are said to be more likely to demand the removal than the addition of materials, and many librarians look upon these demands as individual and spontaneous. A few, however, have noted waves of complaints so similar in nature that they believe they originated with a local diocese. Both public and school librarians who service areas with a high or predominantly Catholic population sometimes are very conscious of this fact as they choose books, whether they themselves are Catholic or not. In the one city of the sample which probably has a small Catholic majority, enough public and school librarians of that faith are employed to warrant the assumption that neither individual nor organized pressures would be necessary to prevent offense to the National Organization for Decent Literature. Similar attention is noticeable in respect to sects such as Mormons, Jehovah's Witnesses, and Seventh Day Adventists in communities where they represent numerically important elements of the population.

All in all, while pressures from voluntary community organizations or institutions may be felt, and while public relations are sometimes looked upon as an increasingly necessary but regrettable interference with professional duties, librarians do not think of these problems as a threat to professional standards or freedom of the library. Even extremist groups whose programs include campaigns to decimate the library are not considered menacing so long as their character is recognized. A more serious problem, as we shall see, is created by persons whose campaigns resemble those of extremist organizations but who claim to be acting independently.

The main difficulty, as both school and public library personnel see it, is that organized groups are not interested in the library at all, except possibly when there is need of a new building. Not one librarian who talked about how he would handle a controversy mentioned a local voluntary organization as a potential source of support. Some said that in the event of such a development they would endeavor to establish *ad hoc* committees (including the clergy and civic leaders) to support library policy, a course adopted in a number of communities which have had controversies over schools or public libraries. No one, however, believed that representatives of any particular community organization should serve on such a committee.

THE PRESS

Despite the proliferation of television stations throughout the state, the growth of educational television stations in certain areas, and the ubiquity of local radio stations, these media were rarely mentioned either as channels of information about libraries or as sources of support or pressure in book controversies. In two metropolitan areas, however, television and radio stations were singled out as having particularly constructive approaches to the public and school libraries. In one of them, the press supported attacks against materials in the school libraries. Several respondents in this community pointed out that radio and television stations had presented the other side of the picture in their newscasts. Otherwise it was invariably the press which appeared to be the key medium.

Keeping the community informed about the policies and objectives of their institutions is a matter of increasing importance to the executives both of public schools and of public libraries. And although discussions of community relations were pertinent in these interviews mainly within the context of controversial materials, most executives shifted focus at some point and talked about public relations in general. In whatever framework public images and expectations of the library were discussed, respondents placed more emphasis on the dissemination of information (or creation of good will) through personal contact with influential citizens and organized groups than through the informational media of the community. This may be due in part to a sophisticated (or intuitive) conviction about the greater effectiveness of personal influence. But there is another factor. The power of the media, particularly of the press, is certainly acknowledged and never belittled; but press policies tend to be viewed as fixed while the attitudes of individuals are looked upon as manipulatable.

Thus, after World War II when local groups in some communities were bent on attacking books or periodicals in the schools or in public libraries, more than one library or school executive felt that his own (sometimes purely social) contacts with the groups concerned had brought about a modification in the attitude of at least some of its members. The situation is different with the press. School administrators or head librarians spoke of local newspapers which do not support the schools or the library, or are perhaps aggressively antagonistic toward them, with an air of defeat. The degree of interest of the local press in school or library, its attitudes toward controversial ideas or materials, and its stand on freedom of expression were viewed as given—unalterable by personal or any other kind of influence. Even where the press was neutral, where there was no antagonism but simply a vacuum, the prevailing attitude was one of futility. The head of a small county library, for example, sought out the editor of the local paper when she was new to her post. His disinterest in the library was immediately apparent. To her observation that she had formerly worked in a community where the press had treated the library as an important institution, he merely turned his back. "But still," she said, "I'd be willing to spend a hundred dollars to get 'public library' mentioned in that paper once a week." A few county librarians were less pessimistic about the press and felt that small newspapers "out in the county" would be receptive to their releases. They had not put the issue to the test, because no member of their staffs had time to supply the copy.

Despite the newspapers' reputation for resoluteness, if not obstinacy, they are seldom reported to be definitely antagonistic to libraries or to the principles for which they stand. In the two communities where extremist groups have conducted the most active campaigns against books and authors, however, librarians and school administrators reported that local newspapers gave the would-be censors active support. In one situation, the publisher of what is locally referred to as an "all-round 'anti' newspaper" had evidently been active, if not actually the generating power, in local Pro-America and Freedom Club groups. This was the only newspaper which was reported to be directly linked to "fringe elements," and in this case there is reason to believe that the paper is more extremist than the organizations whose programs it frequently supports. One of these organizations is reportedly trying to free itself from identification with the paper. A highly censorius member of the library board has gone to great pains to win the approval of a women's club and to reject the enthusiastic but unwelcome support of both the local press and the two restrictive groups.

In more than half of the communities studied, the civic spirit of the press is said to consist mainly of an effort to keep taxes down. Respondents in these communities are inclined to feel that in carrying out this objective the press speaks for business interests which do not necessarily reflect the public interest. Local newspapers are sometimes further described as exploiting sensational episodes or people without presenting enough of the facts for the average reader to make informed judgements.[7] These are common enough descriptions of organs of information which must rely on advertising and reader appeal for subsistence. What they imply, coming from school or library officials, is that the influence of such papers may amount to pressure, if not directly then by default.

People who have campaigned against books in the schools or public libraries have often received wide press coverage, both in their own home towns and elsewhere. Respondents characterize such crusaders as "publicity seekers," pointing out that to complain about library holdings is a sure-fire device for getting into the headlines. This observation was usually made in a rather matter-of-fact fashion. Most administrators and librarians seem to go along with the premise that, in order to sell papers, the press has to sensationalize its reports. They also assume that if a local reporter brings in a list of books attacked in some other community and finds copies of them on the shelves, he will then write a story which will be tantamount to an attack on the library. This assumption holds for those newspapers which have taken editorial stands in support of freedom of the press and freedom to read as much as for those which have not. The ground for this assumption is that the person reading the news item will not necessarily be aware of the paper's stand on such matters unless, as rarely happens, the editorial accompanies the story.

The belief was widespread among our respondents that once a book controversy has arisen the press can play a decisive role in its outcome, but that what the role of a given newspaper would be in such an eventuality could rarely be predicted. It is possibly because of this uncertainty that some school and public librarians who have written book selection policies deliberately avoided sending copies or summaries of them to the press. The only concrete example of press unpredictability was reported about a newspaper whose commitments have never been clear. This incident took place in a community noted for its stability. A local women's organization, rather obviously inspired by someone

---

[7] Among the more notable exceptions pointed out by our respondents is The San Francisco *Chronicle*, which is widely read throughout the northern half of the State. This paper gave thorough and non-sensational coverage to the various book-centered conflicts and episodes throughout the state, together with editorials expressing its own stand on such questions. More recently, it conducted a serious inquiry into the San Francisco Public Library which resulted in a long overdue study of its facilities and services, carried out by a library specialist of national reputation.

from a neighboring town, decided to look into library collections in the local school system. The "campaign" began with an open meeting in which the school officials were confronted with the issue. Several participants in this meeting reported that a local newspaper, whose photographers and reporters came to the meeting and sat through all or most of it, was determined in advance to go along with the need for an "investigation." At the last minute, when it became evident not only that the incipient attack was being sparked by a person from outside the community but supported by "organizers" from extremist organizations (also presumed to live outside of the community), the paper reversed its stand.

Defeatism notwithstanding, heads of municipal and county libraries say they are increasingly aware of the importance of good press relations. Some have acted on this premise by assigning members of the staff to write news articles and releases. Others simply hope that local papers eventually will assign reporters to cover schools or libraries, since they have no one on the library staff qualified (or with sufficient time) to manage publicity. Actually, reports of new acquisitions and of meetings of boards of trustees are, judging from a three-month, state-wide sample of clippings, a matter of course in medium-sized and small communities. In terms of space, it would appear that the public librarian, at least, has little cause for complaint. School libraries, except when there are new buildings or new appointees, are rarely covered in the local press, nor did school librarians or administrators seem to regret this state of affairs.

4

THE ENCOUNTER

Public criticisms of libraries range from the trivial to the traumatic. Patrons, parents, individual crusaders, and organized groups either object to general library policy, or demand removal of (or addition to) material on the shelves. They make their complaints to a desk clerk, a reader's aide or reference librarian, head librarian, school principal, superintendent, school board or library board. The approach may be casual or formal. The person first hearing the complaint may take immediate action or pass it on to someone on another level of the institution. The initial objection is sometimes publicized in a letter to a newspaper, or at an open meeting of a board. More often, the issue does not become a matter of public knowledge at all. From objections that are publicized, partisan episodes occasionally develop. A few have aroused segments of the community not usually concerned with library matters, eventually erupting into community-wide conflicts which were settled only after public hearings, school board elections, or staff dismissals.

Any categorization of the various types of book controversies necessarily underplays their complex and dynamic character; and by presenting those reported by our respondents, we are further handicapped by incompleteness and by blurring of the data. Few of our respondents had direct experience with public episodes or conflicts, and many of the reported events took place some time ago. Despite these shortcomings, there is evidence that under some circumstances a complaint can disrupt a whole community, while under others it may be turned into an affirmation of the positive role of the library.

PATRON COMPLAINTS

The complaints of individual patrons have not changed markedly during the professional careers of our librarians either in respect to the types or numbers of persons making them, or in the nature of the material complained about. There are users of libraries who write critical letters to the head librarian or make critical remarks to the person at the desk about books or authors on moral, religious, ethnic, or political grounds. In school libraries it is more likely to be parents than students who complain about library holdings. Yet even in communities where conflicts over school library books have been highly publicized, no school librarian reported a noteworthy increase or change in parental complaints. Less than 20 per cent came from parents. Only 6 per cent came from students, and they were, for the most part, relaying parental complaints, although a few worried lest a book be harmful to fellow students (table 9). All other objections were from within the school systems—from board members, faculty, administrators, or librarians themselves.

In replying to complaints from patrons or parents, librarians are fairly free to apply their own standards. A few school systems and some of the more centralized public libraries have developed more formal methods; but even with clearly formulated regulations, librarians tend to exercise a large amount of personal discretion. Some schools require all visitors to check in at the principal's office; then he, rather than the school librarian, is likely to hear the complaint. More commonly, the principal does not know the librarian's procedure, and in some schools principal and librarian have developed disparate ways of dealing with complaints. Generally in both public and school libraries the librarian is presumed to have the professional training and experience necessary for meeting complaints.

As may be expected, the largest group of patron and parental complaints reported in this study (about 50 per cent) involved "morals" and profanity (table 10). Typical complaints came from a grandfather who demanded the removal of a book for fear "nice young girls" like his granddaughter would read it, and from middle-aged ladies who murmured about language or morality to assuage their guilt for having read a risqué book. Despite the late Senator Joseph McCarthy's campaign, the program against "un-American" books and authors conducted by the American Legion, the activities of the Tenney Committee and its successors, and the controversy over UNESCO and United Nations materials in Pasadena and Los Angeles, no increase in patron complaints on political grounds was noted. They account for only 22 per cent of the specific objections reported. It is a source of wonder to librarians that politically-oriented book banning campaigns generate so much heat when there seems to be no widespread public anxiety on this score.

Criticisms of library holdings also include requests for the addition of material. In comparison with demands for withdrawals, however, they are insignificant, and most of them lie outside the realm of the controversial. One public librarian did report complaints from members of right extremist organizations that their publications were not available in the library. Another reported pressure from a Communist for the inclusion of Communist literature. Both demands were rejected on grounds that the libraries concerned were not affluent enough to afford the materials necessary to "balance" such acquisitions. Larger systems sometimes accept gifts of political periodicals or pamphlets and, in the case of periodicals, put at least the latest issue on display. Most libraries identify such partisan materials with a gift stamp. One librarian matter-of-factly reported that she also finds the gift stamp a useful device for all controversial publications, donated or not.

Librarians with more generous budgets may accede to such requests. A branch head in a large county library system ruefully reported buying a scurrilously anti-Semitic book under pressure from a member of a Pro-America club. Since the person who demanded that the book be bought had reported keen interest in the volume among members of her club, the librarian anticipated high demand. Actually, it was never checked out. After a time it was taken off the open shelves and put behind the front desk. "At least," this librarian remarked, "if anybody complains that we are not giving all sides of the question, we can show that it's in the catalog."

No marked difference in the pattern of individual complaints is apparent among the various communities included in the study. Reports from librarians in cities which have had publicized book episodes differ in no significant way from those of their colleagues in cities where no such episodes have occurred. The existence of extremist groups or a press which campaigns against certain books or authors has a marked effect on the librarian's own attitudes toward controversial material, but has very little bearing on the kind or number of patron complaints. Nor is the pattern related to size or type of population, although two public librarians believe that their comparative freedom from complaints can be explained by the low educational level of their respective communities. "These people seem to be used to the earthy treatment," was the way one summed up the situation.

Librarians handle individual complaints in a variety of ways. One approach might be characterized as philosophical (or "long-suffering").

At the other extreme is the reactive and restrictive method epitomized by librarians who say, "I just put a book that is complained about away for a while" or, more rarely, "I just burn them." One of the respondents in this latter group went on, in a rather self-pitying way, to ask "Did you ever try to burn a book? It's *very* difficult."

We shall have more to say about the consequences of the various ways of meeting patron complaints, but in passing, a third orientation should be noted. This was one in which the respondent went out of his way to assure the interviewer that there were no public complaints about the holdings of his institution. Such reports were most often made by school administrators or school librarians. In nearly every instance the respondent (or someone else in the same institution) would also emphasize that, in effect, "We have no complaints because we see to it that there is nothing to complain about." Two-thirds of the school personnel reporting "no complaints" have restrictive attitudes toward book selection. No school official or librarian reported "many" complaints, whereas eleven public librarians believed that they did have "many." Concepts such as "many" or "few" are highly relative, of course, and this discrepancy may stem from differences in philosophy as well as from differences in objective situations. More public than school librarians spoke about complaints in the manner of one discussing the daily routine; and unlike school librarians, most public librarians who reported "no complaints" did not have restrictive attitudes toward book selection.

Sixteen patron complaints were recalled as having become matters of official discussion (or controversy) within the ninety-one circulating units covered in the study. Whoever received these complaints referred them to someone else in the institution and they were then taken under advisement, generally by more than one person. Typically the referrals were upward in the institutional hierarchy—a staff member discussing the matter with the head librarian or principal, or, even more frequently, a head librarian taking it up with the board. The majority of complaints thus referred were of a political nature, involving UNESCO, United Nations, other international-relations materials, or the political sympathies or affiliations of an author. Two developed from religious considerations, both of them centering around Paul Blanshard's book *American Freedom and Catholic Power*, but for opposite reasons. One patron borrowed all available copies, "lost," and then paid for them. Another patron accused the librarian of being a Communist because his request for thirty copies of the book, which he wished the librarian to distribute among certain of his friends and acquaintances, was not acted upon.

Ten of the sixteen complaints which reached the level of institutional discussion came from individuals who claimed, or were assumed, to represent organized groups. Eleven of the sixteen occurred in communities where the existence of extremist groups was noted by the respondents. In fact, only one community where extremist groups were reported did *not* have at least one complaint which had developed into an institutional problem. In only three communities where no extremist groups were reported had any patron complaints developed into institutional problems. The same holds true of complaints originating with staff members within a school or library system: they are most likely to be elevated to the level of institutional discussion in communities where there are extremist groups. This is not to say that respondents assumed that these complaints were sparked by extremist organizations. On the contrary, only two were clearly linked with such groups; two others were suspected of a connection with "some fringe group." Apparently the mere presence of an extremist group in the community is conducive to the elevation of a complaint to institutional discussion.

COMMUNITY CONFLICTS AND PUBLIC EPISODES

During the field work of this study only one librarian or school administrator participating in it directly experienced a controversy over books. Judging from press and personal reports, very few of their colleagues elsewhere in the state were so involved during this half year. Two institutions, however, continued to be subjected to long standing and highly publicized pressures.

Book-centered controversies rarely fit neatly into a typology, but for discussion purposes it is convenient to divide them into two categories. *Community conflicts* involve major segments of the population and receive extensive publicity both within the community and outside it. *Public episodes* are generally known within the community but do not involve major segments of the population.

There have been two book-centered community conflicts in the state since the end of World War II. One took place in a city included in this study, the other did not. Both were so well publicized that to describe them anonymously would be a pointless fiction. The first of these received nation-wide publicity. In 1952 the board of education and the school superintendent in the Los Angeles public system were replaced, after a heated battle, on the grounds that the schools' treatment of the United Nations, and of UNESCO in particular, was not education but indoctrination. The attack is assumed to have originated with right extremist groups, and eventually it acquired the support of a number of civic and business groups in the city as well as of the Los

Angeles *Times* and other newspapers. The new board and superintendent saw to it that all UNESCO and much United Nations material was
removed from the school libraries and dropped from the curriculum.
The official resolution of the board (August 18, 1952) specified "permanent withdrawal" of one UNESCO publication only and excluded
adherence to any "UNESCO program," although leaving teaching
"about UNESCO" to the schools. Our Los Angeles respondents reported that the intentions and consequences of this ambiguous declara-
tion were far more restrictive than the wording suggests. A subsequent
board and administration not only continued to act on this mandate,
but expanded it to cover all "un-American" materials, including some
of Dorothy Canfield Fisher's books.

Since the material thus removed had to be replaced, and since (went
the argument) Los Angeles schools are supported by local taxpayers, the
natural substitution was Los Angeles history and its current industrial
and commercial development.

The 150 professional librarians in the school library system found
themselves in a state of confusion as one directive pertaining to policy or
to particular books or authors succeeded another. These directives were
often, and as a matter of principle, delivered orally. Some were formulated extemporaneously to a single librarian who had telephoned headquarters with a question, or to a group of librarians at a meeting. The
result was that librarians in the various schools were never certain as
to what was "permissible" at any given moment. What may have appeared to the public as a conflict settled within a few months became,
for the school librarians in the Los Angeles system, a chronic episode
which lasted for more than five years.[1]

The field work of this study coincided with the Los Angeles school
board election campaign of 1957. Despite announcements and descriptions of the study's objectives in professional journals and bulletins, and
formal clearance with the office of the superintendent, the interviewers
were sometimes hard put to convince school administrators, and occa-

---

[1] The relationship between the school board and the office of the superintendent
in library matters is summarized only briefly here—the full story would require a
separate study of major proportions. It should be noted, however, that since the
completion of the field work of this study, another school board election has been
held and the two most restrictive members of the board have been replaced. Reports indicate that a major liberation of book selection policy is under way, and
the possibility is not remote that the full history of this controversy will now be
told. It was predicted, incidentally, both in Los Angeles and elsewhere, that the
then incumbent school board would prevent the study from being conducted because "it does not like" the Ford Foundation, and, in particular, it does not like
the Fund for the Republic; furthermore, it does not like to have any kind of out-
sider "interfere" with local affairs. (If the Board did take notice of the study, it was
a well kept secret.)

sionally a school librarian, that the study was in no way connected with the campaign. The observation was made that the results would be "biased" because of the election's heat—meaning, presumably, that school personnel would feel more free to speak negatively about the board than they otherwise would. As a matter of fact, they did speak more freely. Some preliminary discussions had been held in the city many months before the election. At that time, restrictive book selection and distribution practices were described as measures designed to "protect the school board," and the interviewer was assured that a member of the system had the choice of going along or resigning. Some of these persons were interviewed again later, when there appeared at least a strong possibility that the two most restrictive incumbents of the board would be replaced. At this time they not only reported their disagreement with board policies in some detail, but described how they had attempted to oppose or circumvent them. The point of this observation is not that the respondents were hypocrites or opportunists, but rather that opposition to the board was being expressed, analyzed, and documented in open public discussion. This free debate in turn served as a releasing mechanism for persons within the system.

The second book-centered community conflict also developed from an attack on school libraries. It took place in 1954 in the Tamalpais Union High School District, Mill Valley. Unlike the rapidly growing and highly heterogeneous city of Los Angeles, this is a small, middle and upper-middle class area. Many writers, artists and musicians, wealthy retired persons, business men, and professional people live in this community. The controversy centered on fifteen allegedly obscene or subversive books, a list which bears a striking resemblance to one used by extremist groups in Texas and elsewhere. Eight of the fifteen books were listed in the 1947 or 1952 editions of the *Wilson High School Catalog*, a publication held in high repute by librarians and educators throughout the country. Of these, four were either "especially" or "doubly" recommended.

This campaign was apparently initiated by one woman, but the county grand jury, and several organized groups in the community quickly became involved, followed by extensive publicity both within and outside the state. A climax was reached during a public meeting of the school district's board of trustees. School librarians and others who were present reported that the tension was so great that the audience screamed when a door slammed in the rear of the room. Neither librarians nor school officials could predict the outcome of this meeting. While it was in progress many participants believed that the campaigner had lined up heavy support from voluntary organizations and community leaders. Actually, of the twenty-five persons who spoke from the floor at the open meeting, nineteen opposed banning the books in question. When one of the members of the board read a strong statement on the freedom to read, concluding with a decision to retain all of the books in question, the hall rang with applause.

Library or book-centered episodes which did not develop into serious community conflicts have been more numerous. Still, only eight were reported by the two hundred persons participating in the study. One of these took place in the early 1930's; six occurred between the end of World War II and 1954; and only one has developed since that time. Judging from the press and from reports made to the Intellectual Freedom Committee of the California Library Association, this pattern seems fairly typical for the state as a whole.

To describe the eight episodes in brief: five stemmed from political objections, two were mainly religious (Roman Catholic), and one was a combined attack against "subversion and pornography." Two county library systems had two each, one municipal library was involved in two, and two school systems each reported one incident. The two religious complaints which developed into episodes originated with library board members; three of those that were politically-centered seem also to have originated with board members, although possibly under pressure from organizations in the community. One, an attack against library sponsorship of an American Heritage Program, was initiated by a right extremist group. Two were instigated by people whose lists of authors and books and whose objectives bear a striking resemblance to those of the Minute Women. (One was the woman who initiated the Tamalpais High School conflict and later tried her wings in another community.) The controversy of the early 1930's, centered on John Steinbeck's *Grapes of Wrath*, is said to have been started by the county board of supervisors. In addition to these eight more or less clear-cut episodes, one other institution in the sample has been subjected to continual attack since World War II. This is the public library already mentioned on which pressure is exerted by a coalition of press, extremist organizations and a member of the board of trustees.

Only four of the more than two hundred persons interviewed in the study had first-hand experience with these episodes: the head of a county system, the head of a municipal system, a school administrator, and a director of libraries in a city school system. In the county system, other staff members were informed but did not participate. The attacks focused on adult education programs and the competence of the chief executive to have the final say in book selection. In the municipal system which became involved in an episode, staff members were informed but not drawn in. The librarian of one of the schools where a public episode was reported by the school administrator had not held the post at the time when it occurred. Librarians in the school system where the director of libraries encountered the neighboring crusader were neither particularly well-informed nor disturbed by the situation. The implication was that they would trust "the boss" to take care of these matters in the best possible way. Both exposure and involvement tended to be at the top.

Do the conflicts and episodes which were settled by the imposition of restrictive measures have anything in common? Are there differences between them which may help explain why one is played out in a low key while the other becomes a threat to community equilibrium?

The Los Angeles school board members and superintendent who were under attack are said to have been neither vigorous nor united in defense of their policies. Moreover, the more powerful newspapers of the area sided with the attackers. In this case the conflict resulted in a defeat for the administration and its policies. The Mill Valley board and administration, on the other hand, united in a vigorous affirmation of their policies. The San Francisco *Chronicle*, which is widely read in the district, supported their stand, and, according to many observers, both the concept of intellectual freedom and the position of those who support it were strengthened in the process. It would take more examples than this to draw firm conclusions, but one might venture the hypothesis that a combination of defensiveness on the part of those attacked and press opposition leads to capitulation to pressures, whereas affirmation of existing policy by those under attack, and press support of their policies, combine to defeat the attackers.

This hypothesis is supported by the example of the community which has not had one isolable episode but is subject to continual pressures for the removal of books or other restrictive measures. Here the public library administration under attack has maintained a forthright and undefensive stand in support of its policies. The local press is on the side of the would be censors. Civic leaders look upon this newspaper as "crackpot" or "extremist." Its statements and restatements of a restrictive point of view, however, may account for the fact that the issues are not settled, but continue to be renewed, first over one book and then another. Or, in terms of our hypothesis, the administration which is under attack for having policies that are too liberal cannot achieve a clear-cut victory because the press supports those who attack its policies.

Among the eight episodes which did not become community conflicts we find certain common factors which may have helped to control them.

In all cases, the administrator whose library policies were under attack matter-of-factly supported them; in none of the eight did the press favor the attackers although, to be sure, they did not give aid or comfort to the administrators being attacked either. Five of these episodes were settled without alteration in policy or a change in personnel; in the other three, the boards advised the administrators to compromise.

Few of the eight episodes were known to librarians or school administrators outside of the community in which they took place. Some were not even known to persons in other institutions within the community. School system personnel in the community where the municipal librarian had recently been embroiled in a publicized controversy with his board, for example, seem to have paid little attention to it or to a similar occurrence a few years earlier. The county librarian, however, whose offices were in the same community, was well informed.

The situation was different in the two community conflicts. Despite the fact that one took place more than five years before this study was undertaken and the other well over three, the majority of respondents throughout the state not only knew of them but brought them into their discussions spontaneously. As we shall see, a number of both school and public libraries reacted to these conflicts with precautionary or restrictive measures. These actions, with very few exceptions, were initiated within the school or library system, without impetus from the local citizenry. Paradoxically the Mill Valley conflict, which was a victory for the freedom to read, was cited as a reason for restrictive practices throughout the state more than the Los Angeles conflict, which was a defeat for freedom in the schools. One explanation for Mill Valley's greater impact may be found in the image and activities of the woman who set it off.

The Censor over the Shoulder

Undaunted by her defeat in Mill Valley, Mrs. X expanded her original list of books and began to campaign throughout the state. Her face was added to her lists as part of her public image when she appeared on Edward R. Murrow's television program. The purpose of this program was to illustrate the kinds of pressures being brought to bear upon the Los Angeles schools. Along with Mrs. X, Murrow interviewed several school librarians (silhouetted for anonymity), a deputy superintendent of the Los Angeles schools, and the Los Angeles County Librarian. The many librarians who saw it felt that except for the remarks of the County Librarian the program did them little credit. The highly dramatized nervousness and anxiety of the librarians, in their opinion, made Mrs. X, by contrast, appear to be both more persuasive and more attractive.

Strengthened by this not too unfavorable publicity (which was certainly not the intent of the program), Mrs. X then went about laying the groundwork for the introduction into the state legislature of a bill which would have allowed almost any degree of censorship in school libraries that local school boards might wish to exercise. The bill, unnoticed by librarians, was unanimously passed by the senate. Later it was soundly defeated in the assembly, after several voluntary organizations and the leaders of the two state professional associations of libraries had become alerted. In the spring of 1957 it was reintroduced, along with several other censorship bills, with substantially the same wording and the same cast of characters. This time "Mrs. X's bill," watered down to the requirement that local school boards prescribe a procedure for the selection and review of all texts and library books, passed both houses but was pocket-vetoed by the Governor.[2]

Mrs. X is widely deprecated by librarians as an emotionally unstable publicity seeker. Yet her name comes quickly to the lips of school and public librarians alike, and her original list of books and authors is well known. One librarian recognized it in the hands of a stranger at the opposite end of a reading room. When plans for the present study were described at a meeting of librarians nearly two years after Mrs. X's initial crusade, one of the first remarks made in the discussion was, "You ought to psychoanalyze her." This was followed, from another part of the room, with, "And librarians, too." Both of these remarks evoked murmurs of agreement from the audience, and taken in juxtaposition they can be interpreted to mean: we fully recognize that there is something irrational in Mrs. X's behavior, and we are concerned because it evokes something irrational in us.

If one opens an inner ear to the undertones of the interviews, the conclusion is inescapable that Mrs. X represents an approach to book selection which librarians find not only distressing but frightening, and they sense that their distress and fright are sharply out of proportion to her "objective" influence. Why this woman, whose campaigns have been marked by failure, has had such an impact is a question that cannot be definitively answered here. But it is tempting to speculate.

The "situation," as Mrs. X presents it, looks like this: there is danger—immorality and subversion—in books. Something must be done about it. One of the places to begin is in the school libraries and she, an educated, devoted mother, is obviously the ideal kind of person to

---

[2] State law already requires school board "adoption" of texts and library books for the elementary level; a 1947 revision of the state education code also requires that district boards "adopt" school library books distributed under contract by the county library and bought out of funds dispensed by the county school superintendent.

undertake the task. Librarians see her furthering this particular cause at the moment but capable of shifting readily to any other—United Nations, group dynamics, fluoridation, or report cards—which might appear more rewarding. Her campaign, ambiguous in itself, triggers ambiguities in those she is directly or indirectly attacking. One respondent summed it up simply: "It's pathetic, but just let somebody raise an American flag over an issue or call forth visions of protecting the American home, and people don't think straight about the heart of the issue."

Hypocritical or not, Mrs. X takes a stand; and the air of conviction with which she does so in itself evokes uncertainties. On the one hand, it is good to speak up for one's principles, as Mrs. X appears to do. On the other hand, unless one is directly attacked isn't it better to keep quiet? "Minor antagonisms may easily set off major disturbances today—like with that woman in Marin County. So it's best to let dead dogs lie." Like most other people, librarians find it easier to be passive than to be active. At the same time librarians are keenly aware of social issues and more idealistic than most about human progress. When they do not stand up to the Mrs. X's they may find themselves in a state of conflict. "It *is* hard to know what to do, you know. We have to serve the district. At the same time we have ideas of what goes into running a library properly, and we have to serve those ideas too."

Librarians also worry lest Mrs. X's apparent upper middle-class façade so impress her listeners that they fail to see through her. This worry may derive from the ambivalence many librarians have about their own professional, and possibly social, status. The strong pride of profession characteristic of most librarians is often matched by anxiety about public stereotypes. The men fear that they are not considered sufficiently virile. The women ask why Bette Davis, in the motion picture, *Storm Center,* was a frustrated, dowdy and middle-aged librarian. Uneasiness about status resulting from the position of the profession of librarianship in relation to other professions enhances these more personal uncertainties. Professional prestige is in part a consequence of the status of the training institution. Schools of librarianship are generally ranked lower in the academic hierarchy and in social status than, for example, schools of medicine or law. No matter how much dignity or pride of profession may be native to or imbued in the librarian, he cannot avoid awareness of this state of affairs. Furthermore, since all librarians doing professional work are not graduates of library schools, there is much uncertainty as to how to define a "professional." Most library leaders believe that eventually all persons with professional functions will have professional training, but some nagging doubts remain about the status implications of the clerical details essential to running a library.

The ambiguities of the image of Mrs. X harbored by librarians may activate conflicts they have about their own image, in much the same way that the neurotic conflicts of two marriage partners nourish each other. The consequences for book selection policy may not be dire, but they are frequently very apparent. The conflict between conviction and doubt may encourage the librarian to turn the basically rational process of book selection into a mystique. The conflict between action and passivity can result in appeasement. Status conflicts may lead to gross overestimates of the amount of public support available for crusaders such as Mrs. X and to equally gross underestimates of the support available to those she wishes to victimize. In the words of one public librarian: ". . . irresponsible people are making all sorts of irresponsible attacks. And what's worse, presumably responsible people are doing the same sort of thing . . . by paying attention to such attacks . . ."

An Atmosphere of Caution

It was not at all unusual, once the librarian had been briefed about the study, for him to jump at once into a discussion of his awareness of caution (his own or other people's) as though he had been waiting for an opportunity to unburden himself. Several felt that the study itself was a rather "courageous" enterprise (a few called it "dangerous") and asked whether there was not a possibility that "someone will clamp down." Some respondents, mainly persons on the staff level in large and highly bureaucratized school or public library systems, recalled that they had felt uneasy when they read about the study in their professional journal and hoped they would not be interviewed. In speculating about the reasons for their feelings of caution, a remark about "this day and age" was not at all infrequent, and some mention of Senator Joseph McCarthy occasionally followed, qualified by a hasty, "I know he has been discredited nationally, but around here . . ." The area "around here" was usually not clearly defined. An alternative explanation was "California has a lot of crackpots, you know." But the respondent's own community was invariably "a literate and broadminded town." There is acute awareness of the climate of opinion, but it is often sensed as something "out there," in some other part of the state.

It may indeed be true that "California has a lot of crackpots." The experiences reported by librarians who have also worked in other states suggest, however, that they are not unique to California. Every state has, or has had, its Mrs. X. The question is not the number of extremists or the nature of their campaigns, but what are the prevalent reactions to them. In this respect, Californians may react just like other people but perhaps more so, because the social changes experienced in other states to varying degrees are, in many areas of California, carried to an extreme which is scarcely conceivable to the mid-Westerner or the New Englander.

The twenty-six communities in which this study was conducted are as diverse in their social as in their geographical characteristics. There are conservative segments of "old" communities which have become more conservative in the struggle to preserve tradition against the influx of new populations. There are sizable cities—mere villages twenty years ago—with little tradition at all. There are towns long characterized by a constrictive triumvirate of press, politics and voluntary groups; and there are communities traditionally conspicuous for courageous newspapers, far-seeing public officials, and an enlightened citizenry.

If the general orientation of the press, city officials, and school and library board members on issues such as civil liberties and intellectual freedom is taken as a rough index of community climate, our sample may be separated into three groups of communities. One is restrictive; another is permissive. In between is a group which for a variety of reasons, not least being rapid economic and population change, is difficult to classify. A common-sense interpretation would suggest that the librarian living in a comparatively uninhibiting atmosphere would feel freer to select controversial materials than the librarian who lives in a constrained community. But this is not true. The most restrictive of our communities have proportionately nearly twice as many non-restrictive librarians as the most permissive (table 11). The community categories were arrived at on too impressionistic a basis to draw definite conclusions, but an analysis of the experiences and practices of librarians who live in an atmosphere charged with threats to civil liberties suggests that they are more likely to feel a sense of responsibility about such issues than are librarians in permissive communities.

More than one librarian was startled during the interviews to hear himself remark that "There's safety in numbers, you know," or "There's no better way to discourage complaints than to insist on having them in writing [in triplicate] and referring them to a committee [or series of committees]." Such statements often prompted the speaker to look at his book selection procedures in a new light. The head of a large public library asked himself whether his delegation of all book selection to a staff committee, justified on the grounds that current output demands more specialization, might not in fact have been motivated by increased circumspection. Others wondered whether the trend toward centralization was not, in fact, the result of an increase in caution rather than an administrative adjustment to growth in school or library systems.

As we have seen, neither librarians nor school administrators explained their feelings of caution by pointing to an increase of direct pressures on their institutions. What strikes them, as they look about in their communities, is not attacks on ideas but the avoidance of them. One librarian noticed that her own young son could find no answer, either in school or in the children's section of the public library, to his question, "What *is* Communism anyway?" Another believes that people feel intimidated by ideas and are, therefore, increasingly fearful of libraries. Events such as the recent last-minute change of a high school radio forum from "Communism and Capitalism in America" to "To Go Steady or Not To Go Steady," because some parents did not wish to have their children discuss the first topic in public, can be reported by nearly every observer of a local scene.

Such avoidance amounts to pressure. Most librarians deplored this state of affairs and recognized its consequences. One head of a municipal library publicly stated at a local meeting that "I thought it was not only proper but a very good thing to have books like that [a history of Russia]. . . . If we're going to fight communism successfully, we have to understand it." But after the meeting an acquaintance warned her to be more careful in her public utterances because one participant in the meeting had picked up the comment as an indication that the librarian was "pro-USSR." She at first shrugged off the warning and told the acquaintance "you can make a Communist out of anybody from some comment or other," but she later observed that "the incident has made me a little more cautious." General caution, or rather, precaution, of this kind is not limited to a few persons or a few institutions. As the next chapter will show, two-thirds of the books mentioned in the interviews as controversial were initially questioned by librarians themselves (and, in school, by faculty members or administrators).

The hush which has fallen over ideological discussion is not restricted to any one political arena or subject field.[3] In talking about

<hr />

[3] Nor is it by any means limited to California. To take just one example, Marya Mannes reports ("Theater: Fancy Fare and Good Home Cooking," *The Reporter*, December 12, 1957): "There was quite a ruckus, you may remember, when the New York Public Library withdrew its sponsorship of the program (reference is to *Faces of War*, written and produced on CBS Television by Harding Lemay—including readings from Euripides, Shakespeare, Cervantes and Twain) in a last-minute

books or authors that have been restricted or removed from their collections, librarians had as much difficulty in remembering names and titles objected to from the right as from the left, and sometimes even references to *Little Black Sambo* and *Huckleberry Finn* were whispered. In extreme cases, librarians may live a nightmare that has strong paranoid undertones:

I have avoided buying [books about Communism] because I do not trust my own judgment. I have traveled a lot . . . I might seem dangerous to some people. They might object to what I bought . . . The public thinks they own their schools and should choose the books.

One committee of school librarians became interested in the question of restrictive pressures on their institutions at about the same time that the present study got under way. They planned a mail-questionnaire survey, and it seemed reasonable to seek some help on questionnaire construction from this study's research staff. After two consultations, the relationship was abruptly broken off, rather clearly to the dismay of the committee on orders from "higher up." The explanation offered to the committee was that, even though the study was being directed from a university, it was known to be supported by a grant from the Fund for the Republic, and "We cannot afford to get mixed up with that group."

Further evidence of how the avoidance of issues in the community at large affects the librarian's own orientation was found among a few respondents who refused to talk about the Los Angeles conflict ("I am a civil servant and might incriminate myself") and among persons who objected to note-taking in the interviews ("In this day and age you don't like people taking down what you say"). Several were reluctant to express their opinions about the Murrow program with Mrs. X and the blindfolded librarians or about *Storm Center* because they are "controversial." As a branch head in a municipal system expressed it: "You have to be careful what you say to people when you have a public job." Two other public librarians decided not to attend a public meeting addressed by Mrs. X. They thought it best not to let themselves be seen—and identified as librarians—by her.

SEMANTIC CONVENIENCES

In the 1930's new or alien political ideologies, including nazism and fascism as well as communism were identified, defined and discussed,

---

spasm of alarm at being involved in a 'sensitive area,' an argument for peace being not, as one trustee was quoted as saying, 'in the public interest.' It was public interest, in fact, that brought the library back to its fundamental senses: the board expressed regret at its withdrawal and indicated a new awareness of the powers of TV for good."

not only by scholars but in the press, on the radio, and in schools and colleges. Those who opposed such ideologies could sometimes cite chapter and verse explaining why they considered them dangerous. Today nondemocratic ideologies evoke anxiety. There is worry about the fact that they exist, but no very concrete idea of what in particular makes them dangerous. Anything which seems potentially troublesome is simply dumped into the witches' brew labeled "controversial" or "un-American." A book or an author complained about by any person for any reason may, quite legitimately, be called controversial. The fact that this term can be applied to a work is often taken to mean that it is "bad." The pros and cons of controversy are forgotten in the stress on the *con* in controversial.

School is supposed to provide the basic equipment and information necessary for responsible citizenship. . . . I suppose it's probably heresy, but that's why I think it's important to teach about Communism and have books about Communism. . . . Maybe the reason people are so excitable today [about the threat of Communism] is because they don't have the [intellectual] equipment and information necessary for dispassionate, mature behavior . . .

The tendency toward blanket rather than specific criticism is reflected in the nature of public concern with library books, or at least that part of public concern which appears to be organized. Authors, rather than works, are indicted, and the indictment is often general and undocumented. "Usually there's really no proof. . . . Just being accused seems to be equated with guilt." Such imprecision is at times confounded by witting or unwitting obliqueness. Many complaints, for example, focus ostensibly on pornography or obscenity but may very well spring from motives or prejudices having little to do with either. Such tactics are particularly convenient when the real motives or prejudices of the objector might be interpreted as in themselves un-American (e.g., racial or religious prejudices). They sometimes result in a kind of shadowboxing between the alleged prejudices of the objector and the susceptibilities of the librarian. Librarians recognize that however well developed their critical sense may be in literary matters, their personal sensibilities are often near the surface where they can be tapped all too easily. Some have had to work particularly hard to overcome their personal distaste for the sexual material common to much contemporary writing, especially when it seems to be introduced more for sales appeal purposes than as an intrinsic part of what the author has to say. It is with a sense of irony that they realize that some would-be censors simply utilize sex passages as a pretext. Many books are ignored altogether which are fully as "erotic" or "pornographic" or "obscene" as those which are attacked, and an examination of the controversial books often shows that they have something other than sex in common, such as a sympathetic treatment of race relations.

Similar examples of displacement are apparent in attacks ostensibly made on political grounds. Many books at least as sympathetic to Communist ideas as Pearl Buck's and Eslanda Robeson's *American Argument* is presumed to be appear in the publications lists of the past fifteen years. But it is this one book, suggesting a working relationship between members of two races, which has been singled out for attack by library critics. Objections to UNESCO materials in school libraries may have similar origins. The stated complaint is that these materials are un-American because they are too sympathetic to Communist countries, or because they imply the necessity of surrendering some of America's sovereignty. A closer look reveals that they also present the lowering of racial barriers in a favorable light.

It is not only the word "controversial" which is laden with emotional affect. "To censor," in all of its variations, and the word "pressure" are disliked or avoided by many of our respondents. "Why," asked a county library department head, "do you keep referring to pressure groups? To the public librarian, all groups are pressure groups." Words deriving from "to censor" were avoided not only in connection with a given librarian's own practice of book selection (sometimes clearly censorial) but in more abstract discussions of library philosophy. Librarians "screen," "select," and "guide." As a librarian in a large municipal library put it, "We haven't been censoring but we have been 'conservative'. After all, this is a conservative community, and that is how parents here want it to be." But, ruminated a few, when we take actual or potential controversiality into account in the screening, selecting and guiding, are we not indeed censoring? Others do not ask; the word is avoided. Selection which by-passes the controversial is justified by use of the same terms of opprobrium used by would-be censors. In speaking of contemporary works of fiction, one municipal librarian reported her views as follows: "If they are out-and-out obscene they should not be in the library at all . . . [but] 'touchy' books . . . have a legitimate place in the public library. . . . [However] since some people do find them objectionable, they are kept on reserve." Or, as another public librarian said: "You have to screen the organizations that want to put on exhibits because you don't want any 'neo-Communists' in the library. You also have to make sure there is nothing in the exhibits that might be considered controversial."

Such remarks, which were by no means infrequent in the interviews, were often followed by some such observation as "this means that we now have a good deal of freedom, you see." What these librarians seem to mean is that institutions having "conservative" policies are not as likely to attract public attention. Public attention sometimes results in community controversy and community controversy sometimes results in restrictive measures. Then you *really* have restrictions. This is the same line of reasoning that led some of our respondents to accuse those who have been involved in public episodes of using the wrong language. If, say these critics, the administrator or the school librarian had said, "We've called those books in for review," rather than, "We've withdrawn them," the segment of the public which is opposed to restrictive practices would not have become aroused, the restrictors would have been pacified, and no episode would have developed.

Some librarians have adopted an even more positivistic semantic philosophy, much of which is formally sanctioned in library policy and training. There is little talk of avoiding the controversial, or even of being conservative; rather, library materials must be in "good taste," they must be "suitable" or they must be "appropriate." In school libraries or library systems, the equivalent is likely to be the irreproachable statement, "Our materials must supplement the curriculum." The less sanguine school librarian adds "and everyone knows that the curriculum, after all the commotion about textbooks, is pure!"

5

ACTION AND REACTION

The discrepancy between theory and practice in book selection is often attributed to a time lag in the adaptation of professional philosophy to social change.[1] The resulting gap is one which the elements of public opinion or of private temperament are all too ready to fill. The philosophy of the profession as it applies to controversial books is felt to be particularly inadequate; the consequence is a rather dramatic inconsistency between attitudes and behavior.

Nearly one-half of the librarians interviewed in this study expressed unequivocal freedom-to-read convictions. The rest were divided between those whose doctrine is clearly restrictive and those who express weak, wavering, or contradictory opinions. On the verbal level, county librarians are far freer than others; 72 per cent expressed strong freedom-to-read convictions, and only 5 per cent reported restrictive doctrines (table 12). Among all librarians, those with professional training were more likely to give verbal support to the freedom to read than those without training. The highest proportion of persons with restrictive attitudes (one-third) is found among those with no professional training at all (table 13).

When it comes to actual practice, nearly two-thirds of all librarians who have a say in book selection reported instances where the controversiality of a book or an author resulted in a decision not to buy. Nearly one-fifth *habitually* avoid buying any material which is known to be controversial or which they believe might become controversial

---

[1] Similar ideological lags were being observed at least two decades ago. Cf. Clarence E. Sherman, "The Definition of Library Objectives" in C. B. Joeckel, ed., *Current Issues in Library Administration* (Chicago: University of Chicago Press, 1939).

(table 14). Among those who expressed strong freedom-to-read convictions, 40 per cent take controversiality into account under some circumstances, particularly if another, more "legitimate," reason can be found for avoiding a book. For example, if it can be condemned as "literary trash" or, in the case of school librarians, if it can be described as on "too advanced a reading level" (table 15), the volume will not be ordered. County librarians account for much of the discrepancy between verbal attitudes and behavior: 72 per cent expressed strong freedom-to-read convictions, but only 37 per cent do not take controversiality into account in actual book selection. The difference between the verbal and actual behavior of municipal librarians is noticeable but not dramatic. School librarians are somewhat freer in actual behavior than in verbal expression, a fact which is probably related to their special working conditions. Librarians whose verbal attitudes were restrictive were more consistent. The majority habitually avoid controversial material, and there is not one who does not take controversiality into account under some circumstances. People with contradictory, wavering, or weak attitudes are sometimes less restrictive in actual practice than their words would suggest. More than one-third of them, mainly people who work in large systems, gave no evidence of taking controversiality into account. Like some school librarians, they may have feared that their words would be held against them, while their comparatively free practices are obscured by many layers of bureaucratic decisions.

It is doubtful whether many librarians would agree that consistency is always a virtue in book selection, but it is also doubtful whether many are quite aware of the extent of their inconsistencies in buying controversial books. The librarian who has President Eisenhower's statement on freedom to read pasted on the glass door of a locked bookcase is probably not conscious of anything untoward about this circumstance. The one who burned a book on "that woman's list" may be somewhat more aware of the inconsistency of her act with her stated allegiance to the Library Bill of Rights, because she found it necessary to rationalize her action. "You do not jeopardize a whole institution just for one book." This is by no means an uncommon rationalization. More often than not the "just one book" (or author or group of books or authors) is eventually joined by many others. Persons who react in this way tend to do so rather indiscriminately. It does not matter who the complainant is or what the complaint is about. The way to handle the situation is to "just put it away for a while." The duration of the "while" was never voluntarily specified, but further questioning revealed that it often meant indefinitely.

About 2,000 of these "just one" books which were temporarily put aside have found their way into the back room of one public library.

THE ROLE OF CONTROVERSIALITY

There are two stages at which a librarian's practices in regard to controversial materials become manifest: in the act of book selection itself, and in circulation procedures.

School librarians tend to be most conscious of controversiality at the time they make decisions about new purchases—29 per cent of them habitually avoid controversial material in making selections, as contrasted with 5 and 17 per cent of the county and municipal librarians, respectively (table 14). On the other hand, a somewhat higher proportion of school librarians does not take controversiality into account at all in making their initial selections. They are more likely to follow consistently free or consistently restrictive patterns, whereas municipal librarians tend to cluster in the middle ground, avoiding controversial material if it is compatible with a "legitimate" reason. Such avoidance, however, is not always consistent or complete. The librarian who is highly demand-oriented, for example, may reverse a decision in the light of public request. "We decided not to get *Peyton Place* because it sounded so purely sensational, but there's been such a great demand that we'll probably end up buying a few copies. A decision not to buy is never final; no matter how controversial a book may be, if there is great and persisting demand among responsible patrons, it eventually gets bought. You might say we use a delaying tactic."

County librarians, perhaps because of the ease with which books can be transferred from one branch to another in the event of complaint, are not so inclined to avoid controversial material habitually as are school and municipal librarians. Among librarians who do not take controversiality into account at all, the differences are not nearly so sharp. Proportionately as many school as county librarians are in this category, with municipal librarians falling somewhat behind.

At first glance, the comparatively greater freedom of some school librarians may appear rather surprising. Most of the attacks on library books to date have been directed against school libraries; furthermore, school librarians have reasons widely acknowledged as legitimate (such as reading level and the necessity to supplement the curriculum) for avoiding material. Actually, their freedom is probably more apparent than real. The budget, the clientele, and the more narrowly construed role of the school library limit their range of choice. School librarians may have to make decisions about *Citizen Tom Paine* or the works of Mark Twain, but rarely about *American Freedom and Catholic Power* or *Peyton Place*.

A school librarian working in a metropolitan system is not as likely to order controversial material as is a school librarian in a smaller city (table 16). Not size of city itself, however, but degree of bureaucratization seems to be the decisive factor here. Librarians in independent schools in metropolitan areas may not take controversiality into account, while practices in centralized multi-school districts covering many small towns tend to resemble those in large cities.

Whether a book-centered public episode has occurred locally or whether the librarian perceives the flow of patron complaints as "many" or "few" seems to have little bearing on the restrictiveness of attitudes or practice. Nor does the rate of growth of a community seem to be a factor which has any bearing on the caution a librarian exercises in selection. The composition of the population, however, appears to have some significance. Nearly one-half of the librarians who live in communities which are comparatively homogeneous in regard to ethnic factors do not take controversiality into account in selecting books, compared with one-fourth of those in heterogeneous communities (table 17). Among school librarians, the effect of mixed populations seems to be most noticeable.

. . . the feeling is that everybody is a member of some sort of minority, and each minority feels it has to scramble and scratch to preserve itself and to assert its standards. . . . Having lots of groups like this makes people more sensitive and reflects in policies and operations, and therefore on book selection.

With behavior as with attitudes, training, experience, and professional affiliations generally are more pertinent factors than are pressures from patrons, local groups, or other community influences of which the librarian may be aware. Persons with professional training in librarianship are more likely to disregard controversiality in selecting library materials than are those without it—41 per cent of the professionally trained as compared with 29 per cent of those who are not (table 18). Those with no professional training are more likely to avoid controversial materials habitually (29 per cent as compared with 16 per cent). In view of the greater tendency, or necessity, of school librarians to adapt their policies to those of their principals or library supervisors, it is not surprising that among them professional training is less decisive. Two professionally trained school librarians habitually avoid controversial materials for every three who do not take controversiality into account, whereas among professionally trained public librarians the ratio is one to five (table 19).

Among public librarians, the location of the school where professional training was received has little bearing on whether they take controversiality into account in book selection. Among school librarians place of training does play some role. Those who received a library degree or certificate in California tend to avoid controversial material. Those trained elsewhere tend not to take controversiality into account (table 20).

Even more decisive than professional training is length of work experience. Librarians relatively new to the profession tend to be much less restrictive than their more experienced colleagues. Fifty-six per cent of the people who have worked less than ten years do not take controversiality into account in book selection, compared with only 24 per cent among those who have worked twenty years or more. At the other extreme, 24 per cent of those who have worked twenty years or more habitually avoid controversial material in book selection compared with 15 per cent among those who have worked fewer than ten years (table 21). At first thought, this discrepancy might seem to be accounted for by lack of professional training among older librarians. This is not true. Persons who have worked thirty or more years are just as likely to have professional training as those who have worked fewer than ten (table 22).

The group falling between the two poles of habitual avoidance and never taking controversiality into account consists of more than 40 per cent of the librarians interviewed. These are primarily the people who avoid controversial books if some "professional" justification can be found for such avoidance. A few reject material which is currently in the spotlight, regardless of whether any other justification for such avoidance can be found. The role of activity in professional library organizations is particularly striking in connection with this middle-range group. One-half of the librarians who are active in local, regional, state, or national professional organizations fall in this category, avoiding the controversial if it is in the spotlight or if a reason based on "standards" can be found (table 23). Non-joiners, on the other hand, tend not to take controversiality into account. Middle-range behavior is also somewhat more common among those who read the professional journals most avidly (table 24). By design or by accident, exposure to professional organizations seems to be conducive to the kinds of compromises in book selection that can be professionally rationalized.

REMOVALS AND RESTRICTIONS

Restrictions are placed on the circulation or distribution of controversial books in 82 per cent of the ninety-one circulating library units covered in this study (table 25). Nearly one-third reported that controversial materials have, on one occasion or another, been permanently removed from their collections. The most frequent forms of restriction are transfer to the librarian's office (33 per cent of all institutions reporting); placing on "reserve" so that the patron must request the book (33 per cent); and placing under or behind the front desk (27 per cent). Less frequent are restrictions by means of limiting the number of copies purchased (15 per cent), and placing material in locked cases (7 per cent). When the book remains on the premises the card is invariably left in the catalog.

Caution at the point of selection limits the need for caution in circulation. It is not surprising, therefore, to find that thirteen of the seventeen units reporting no restrictions in circulation were school libraries. Not only are there more public libraries which restrict the circulation of material, they exercise more types of restriction as well. School libraries reported an average of one and one-half kinds of restrictions each, whereas public units reported an average of more than two. Permanent removal of a book after purchase is also reported more often in public than in school libraries.

School librarians most frequently resort to the device of placing restricted books in the librarian's office (occasionally, in the nurse's office), to be circulated at his or her discretion. Public librarians are most likely to restrict books by placing them on a reserve shelf or keeping them behind the front desk. Books so placed must be specifically requested by the patron, but, unlike the books in the office of the school librarian, they are generally visible.

How these various forms of restraint come about can best be traced from librarians' descriptions about how they handle particular patron complaints. As we have already noted, several hundred references to books or authors were made in the course of the interviews. No one book or author was mentioned more than twenty-six times, and the vast majority were mentioned only once or twice; altogether, about 150 different titles were mentioned, and occasionally authors without specification of book. The most frequent references included *Peyton Place* (26 respondents), *The Ninth Wave* (15), various Felson titles (11), various Fast titles or all his books generally (10), *From Here to Eternity* (9), *What is Communism* and *What Is Democracy* (7), *Grapes of Wrath* (6) or Steinbeck generally (6). Others mentioned more than twice include *The Naked and the Dead* (5), *American Freedom and Catholic Power* (5), *Being Born* (4), Karl Marx' works (4), *Memoirs of Hecate County* (4), the two Kinsey reports (4), Dorothy Canfield Fisher's "later books" (4), *Gone with the Wind* (3), *American Argument* (3), *Senior Spring* (3), *Ideal Marriage* (3), *Ulysses* (3), *The Nun's Story* (3), *Blackboard Jungle* (3), Galt's "UN book": *How the United Nations Works* (3), *Forever Amber* (3), Richard Wright or *Pagan Spain* (3), Langston Hughes generally (3).

These examples were usually offered by the respondent in order to clarify his viewpoint or to describe the kinds of complaints he receives and how they are treated. Well over two-thirds were books questioned by librarians themselves, or, in the case of school libraries, by librarians, administrators or teachers, without any stimulation from complaints of patrons or parents (table 9). Decisions not to purchase, or to restrict circulation, were made in 72 per cent of all cases reported. The distribution of restrictive actions resembles the complaint pattern (tables 10 and 26), except for school librarians who cite political grounds about twice as often as the sex-morality complex, despite the fact that only two of the parental complaints reported were of a political nature.

Books complained about by patrons or others outside the institution were by no means as likely to result in restrictions or removals as were those questioned by librarians themselves or by others within their institutions; in fact, 56 per cent of the outside complaints were resisted. (Public librarians are more likely to react restrictively to external complaints than are school librarians.) Of the controversial material questioned from within, 85 per cent was removed or otherwise restricted (table 27). School and public librarians closely resemble each other in their reaction to colleague- or self-initiated problem books.

Caution, then, is exercised not so much in reaction to local public opinion as in reaction to seemingly self-generated problems. It would seem that the more direct and severe the pressure from the community, the firmer the resistance. Recall, for a moment, the eight public complaints which turned into episodes. Five were resisted by the librarians and were soon resolved without change in policy or removal of controversial material. Two, on the advice of the board, were not resisted by the librarian; but these episodes focused on matters of administrative policy, rather than on controversial books. *The Grapes of Wrath* episode in the early 1930's resulted in removal (also on advice of the board), but the book has long since returned to the collection.

We find a similar refusal to capitulate to local pressure in regard to the public complaints which came to involve discussions among various levels of the institution concerned: restrictive action was taken in only five of the sixteen situations reported (three of these five complaints were made to school librarians who discussed them with their principals or library supervisors and were told to remove the book in question).

Quite in contrast to this resistance to local pressures, restrictive measures were introduced in twelve institutions as a direct result of the community conflicts in Los Angeles and Marin County. Ten of these institutions were schools or school systems. In seven of them the restrictive action was initiated by the administration (principal, curriculum coördinator, or "someone" in the office of the superintendent).

One school principal told the interviewer that "of course" he immediately checked his library and ordered all books on Mrs. X's list removed, explaining that he was shocked to find they had been included in his library's collection in the first place. "Even you, a mature reader," he told the interviewer, "would blush if I read you her list of quotations." In another community, a school librarian reported that her principal (who did not wish to be interviewed) had been alarmed about the Marin affair. A subsequent check of news releases unearthed a newspaper report from a neighboring city quoting him as saying that any book complained of in that episode would be removed if found in the library of his school. The librarian reported that, although so far as she knew not a single local parent had reacted to the Marin conflict. A newspaper reporter had checked the list against the holdings of all high schools in the community; it was this action which had set off the alarm, although the paper has a reputation for supporting libraries, civil liberties, and intellectual freedom. A second high school principal in the same city went with the reporter to check his school library and found none of the fifteen books. The librarian in this school, incidentally, had reported that whenever a complaint is made about a book she removes it to a room inaccessible to students. There are now about thirty books in this room. In a third community, the principal of a high school spent a full morning going through old accessions lists the day after he heard of the Marin County affair. Upon finding none of the controversial books, he said that he supposed not even the most avid newspaper reporter would go back more than ten years.

Respondents in three schools reported that since the UNESCO conflict, materials on the United Nations and UNESCO had been removed or are "no longer promoted." A great many more reported that students and teachers now make much less use of any UN material that is available. "They never," said one school librarian, "seem to reach that part of the book any more." Several librarians, usually at the insistence of their principals, have put the books on Mrs. X's list on "parental permission only." This means that they are given only to students who have their parents' written approval to withdraw them. The "parental permission" technique has been adopted in two school systems for all books the librarian suspects might become problematic in any way.

In the remaining schools where restrictive measures were introduced as a result of the conflicts in Los Angeles and Marin County, teachers seem to have taken the initiative without administrative sanction. One teacher removed several books from the school library after seeing the Murrow program; another removed a book by Owen Lattimore. Few school librarians reported that they had restricted or removed such materials on their own initiative. There is also little indication that they opposed the restrictive measures taken by their administrators or fellow faculty members. The one school librarian who did resist pressure from a vice-principal to remove a book won out—with the help of a friend who happened to be a member of the school board.

The only two instances of pressure on schools exerted by local citizens as a result of the Los Angeles or Marin County conflicts evoked what might be called semi-resistance. In one community, a woman approached the school board with Mrs. X's list. The school board wavered but finally, due to the persuasiveness of an eminent local clergyman, decided to drop the matter. At the same time, however, this board decided that a written book selection policy was in order. (One librarian in this system reported that school principals had received instructions from the superintendent's office to "go over every book in their libraries.") In the second community, a grand jury member, with the permission of the principal, personally removed one of the books on Mrs. X's list from the high school library. This story was reported by an official in the office of the superintendent of schools, who pointed out that the principal concerned had been "put on the carpet" for allowing this removal, and that eventually the book was retrieved for the collection.

The two restrictive reactions to Los Angeles or Marin County reported from public libraries were initiated by librarians themselves, but on a rather unofficial basis. A librarian in charge of a county library's young adult collection removed all material on the USSR after the Los Angeles conflict, presumably without consultation with her superior. The head of a municipal library in another community decided that "we should stay away from Langston Hughes for a while."

Counting both official and unofficial moves, restrictive reactions to the Los Angeles and Marin County conflicts were reported by eighteen of the twenty-six communities covered in the study. There is no apparent relationship between proximity to the communities where these two conflicts took place and reaction to them. In fact, more institutions located in the central or northern parts of the state removed UN and UNESCO materials as a result of the Los Angeles conflict than did those in the South; and southern as well as northern communities reacted to the Marin County episode. Six of the eight communities reporting no reaction were of less than 25,000 population. Two of these are made up of low and low-to-middle socio-economic groups where it is mainly public school students who use the libraries, and parents have little interest in schools or libraries. The rest have grown so rapidly in the last five years that, as one librarian explained, no one has time to think about anything but how to expand facilities to meet the growing needs of the town. One of the two cities of more than 25,000 population where no reaction to these conflicts was reported is also growing very rapidly and has had a high turnover of population since the war. The chief complaint of librarians and school administrators in this city was that there is no stable element which takes an interest in any community institution.

The second larger city untouched by the Los Angeles and Marin conflicts is comparatively old, stable and homogeneous. Its citizens have long maintained a high level of civic and cultural activity. School administrators and public librarians there describe their boards as distinguished, and their functions as traditional: interpreting the institution to the community and protecting the institution from destructive or vicious elements. Heads of all institutions covered in this community were active participants in community organizations. The newspaper supports civil liberties and intellectual freedom issues, and its editor, a member of the library board for a number of years, was referred to by the head librarian as "a man of great vision" in respect to his conception of the role of the library in the community.

ADMINISTRATIVE ESCAPES, SOLUTIONS, AND RESOLUTIONS

Library executives differ in the intensity of their concern with book selection problems. Among those who appear to be relatively uninterested in book selection, two groups are distinguishable. First, librarianship, like any profession, has its quota of people whose orientation is largely administrative or technical. For some head librarians buildings, finances, annual reports, procedures, and staff relationships are all-important. Most executives of this type seem to respect books, even though they are not personally interested in them. A few may sweep away a book that has been an object of controversy or of uneasiness in the same matter-of-fact fashion as they would sweep away a bid from a rascally contractor.

The other type of executive who seems mainly concerned with administrative at the expense of substantive matters appears to be reacting—possibly without knowing it—to the problems and pressures of book selection. It is among this group that there is some evidence of escapism, of the substitution of procedures for principles, or of so intense an absorption in techniques that there is little time left for the consideration of objectives.

A similar rough typology may be developed for school administrators. Because of their many other responsibilities, they cannot be expected to have much time for book selection problems. But here again we find people who are predominantly interested in substance and content; those who, as a matter of training and disposition, are more concerned with procedure; and others who seem to escape in administrative matters as a means of avoiding complex or controversial problems. Unlike the library executives interviewed, only a minority of school administrators are oriented principally toward content—a situation no doubt in part accounted for by the fact that nine of the twenty-two administrators who furnished information about their professional experience were former coaches, physical education or shop teachers.

This is not to underestimate the importance of administrative competence, nor to imply that routinized procedures for handling complaints or other types of controversies have no practical or moral value. On the contrary, there is evidence that in matters of book selection, as in many other matters of principle falling within the scope of the library or school administrator, a careful formulation of policy and procedure may help the staff members to clarify their thinking and possibly help the board or the public to understand the function of the library in the community and in the school.

The most frequently discussed administrative aid for problems of controversiality is the written book selection policy. As we have already noted, the Los Angeles and Marin conflicts provided impetus for the development of such policies in both public and school libraries. Prior to the Los Angeles conflict in 1954, only two of our school systems and one public library had written policies. By the spring of 1956, after the Marin conflict, four school and six public libraries had adopted such policies. A year later four more school and nine more public libraries had either completed them or were in the process of doing so. Respondents in nine systems (six school, one municipal, and two county) stated that their policies were drawn up as a direct result of the Los Angeles and Marin conflicts.

Originally, the initiative for the preparation of such statements for the schools came largely from the administration (sometimes at the instigation of the school board). After the Marin County conflict, however, school librarians, stimulated by the activities of an *ad hoc* committee of the School Library Association of California, Northern Section, played a much more active role. This committee was also established at least in part as a consequence of Mrs. X's activities. It collected book selection policies [2] from school libraries throughout the state, analyzed and evaluated them, and reproduced a number for distribution to school administrators and librarians. The project was undertaken with the material help, although not the moral support, of the California Teachers' Association (of which the School Library Association is an affiliate). At about the same time, local, regional, and state groups of public librarians began to discuss the pros and cons of written policies. A number of model statements were circulated among municipal or county libraries. Many school librarians felt that their professional organization strongly encouraged the development of written policies. The picture was not so clear to public librarians.

The methods of drawing up book selection policies vary. In some school systems and public libraries the entire professional staff, occasionally working with their respective boards, thrashed out every detail. More frequently, one or two persons (head librarian or assistant librarian, assistant superintendent or curriculum coördinator) prepared the policy and presented a draft to the staff for suggestions. In a few cases, policies were taken over almost verbatim from other institutions.

There is also little uniformity in what happens to policies after they have been completed. Official adoption by the board is increasingly common. Two-thirds of those completed prior to the field work had been given official sanction. A few librarians keep copies at hand for ready reference. More often, the policy has simply been filed. A number of librarians reported that they did have written book selection

---

[2] The American Library Association and the California State Library have long advocated written book selection policies, but not for defensive purposes.

policies but could not find them, had forgotten who prepared them, and had little idea what they contained. Occasionally, both in school and public libraries, some staff members had no idea of the existence of these documents, even when they constituted official regulations.

With such a variety of methods of formulation and use, it is not surprising that librarians disagree as to the efficacy of written policies. Although the majority of the institutions which have adopted them did so as a protective measure, two-thirds of our librarians have doubts about their usefulness. Fifteen public and five school librarians believe that they have no protective value at all; and a few of these believe that written policies may do more harm than good.

Disagreement as to their efficacy stems largely from different concepts of the power of the written word. There are people who say that if there is a policy in writing the public will realize how conscientious they are. Others believe that the safest book selection policy consists of never putting anything in writing. Somewhere between are those who say: I have no written policy because my fingers haven't been burned yet. The two extremes are occasionally found in the same institution. A system having written statements of general policy may at the same time have an unwritten policy never to mention a particular book or author in writing. The result is, as one staff member observed, that a remark by a higher authority at a staff meeting to the effect that certain books or authors have become "questionable" may be interpreted as an order to remove or restrict the material.

Institutions having policies which were not intended to serve as protection are, for the most part, the larger public libraries. In these institutions the development of a detailed book selection policy for training purposes has long been traditional procedure. Librarians who have these policies are quick to point out that they are the only kind that can help the librarian in his task of book selection, and that a policy instrument which is helpful for the staff cannot possibly be used for public relations purposes.

In addition to the disagreement about the utility of written policy for public relations there is also disagreement about the degree of specificity which any kind of written policy should have. An analysis of the policies themselves suggests that the people in favor of generalities won out.

Among the thirteen public and seven school policies completed are one blanket adoption of the Library Bill of Rights (which could not be found), one "staff policy" (used as a buffer against the board), and two statements which have never been duplicated for staff distribution. The school statements include two which have been incorporated into the district education code, one which is an edict from the office of the superintendent. In almost all instances, the broad postulation of "objectives" is given the most space and weight. Sometimes objectives are formulated as if they were synonymous with standards for selection; when standards are spelled out at all, they are as likely to consist of criteria for excluding material from a collection as of criteria for inclusion, and both sets of criteria permit a wide range of subjective interpretation. "Author's intent," for example, is offered as a significant criterion, without specifying how such intent is to be determined, or who is qualified to determine it. Similarly the statement that "all sides" of controversial issues will be represented is recurrent, without any indication of how the controversial is to be defined. Standards, when mentioned at all, have much more to do with the presumed effects of books than with their qualities. Only one policy statement explicitly rejects public opinion as a criterion for either inclusion or exclusion of a book in the collection. Only one unequivocally affirms the duty of the public library to promote communication and stimulate controversy, "whether [the books] are recognized classics or [are] innovations in ideas, format or literary form." This statement is unique both in its specificity and in lack of evasiveness on the subject of controversial materials.

Two of the written policies spell out how public complaints should be met. There are, however, both school and public libraries which have adopted standardized, though unwritten, complaint procedures. These range from a requirement that complaints be referred to the principal or head librarian to an elaborate system of "discouragement by committee." Four schools or school systems have established standing committees to receive complaints, committees which are usually made up of faculty members, an administrator and a librarian. The method consists of requesting the complainant to put his objection in writing, citing chapter and verse, and to submit it in triplicate. He is informed that his objection will be reviewed by the standing committtee; that if this committee does not agree, an *ad hoc* committee will be established to review the problem; if it in turn cannot come to a decision, the matter will be referred to the school board.

All standing committees for the review of complaints were dormant at the time of the study. In one large school system, three headquarters professionals (an assistant superintendent, the library supervisor, and the chairman of the central book selection committee) gave three different versions of the membership and function of the complaint committee. Most operating school personnel interviewed in the system were unaware of its existence.

Procedures in public libraries are less systematized. In large metropolitan systems where book selection is centrally coördinated, the branch librarian is likely to refer all complaints to headquarters, just as the school librarian in a large school system tends to refer complaints to the office of the superintendent. Similarly, in public libraries where the head librarian tends to be authoritarian in the management of the library, the subordinate librarian who receives a complaint is likely to refer the complainant to "the boss." This is believed to be a deterrent particularly in instances where the head librarian is a prominent member of the community—but few examples of its efficacy were offered. One person who complained about book selection policy in a large city library was asked to submit his objection in writing and took up the challenge in flowery style, setting off a series of time-consuming meetings starting with a small staff committee but eventually involving the entire board of trustees.

Formal techniques for routing complaints tend, like written book selection policies, to be evasive, despite the fact that they are often thought to be effective substitutes for a positive approach, or even to comprise a positive approach. Although such procedures receive enthusiastic support from some administrators, the evidence from this study suggests that direct action, without recourse to written policy or "complaint procedure," not only saves time, but is less likely to result in restrictive measures.

Another less widespread device for forestalling or alleviating public complaints is the use of the "tools" as buffers. Many librarians, as we have seen, feel that they are becoming, of necessity, more dependent on book reviews in the book selection process. About one-tenth of the librarians covered in this study use these tools as safety devices against actual or potential complaints. But even among those who do use reviews for this purpose, there is little agreement as to how they should be used. One public librarian, for example, reported that a book is controversial if the reviews disagree and that such a book receives special attention, sometimes with restrictive results. In one school system, a book is not bought unless all major reviews which this particular system draws upon agree about it. In another, the book selection "policy" is not to buy a book unless at least one standard professional review approves it. Book awards are also occasionally referred to for support. Public librarians, particularly those in non-metropolitan communities, are more likely to use reviews as a justification of avoiding purchase of the controversial books or as a means of justifying one that is complained about. The former practice is the more frequent, and the source most frequently relied upon is the book review service of Virginia Kirkus. Three municipal libraries never buy a book if a Kirkus review raises a warning flag.

Reaction to anticipated difficulties is not always specific. It may simply result in a kind of generalized precaution exercised in the selection process or in the public rooms of the library itself. Many of our respondents, for example, reported a heightened awareness, of new purchases for "young adults," and this awareness is extended to the reading rooms. Sometimes books deemed harmless for the teenager are placed on shelves labeled in such a way as to attract his attention. The browsing youth is watched rather more carefully than he used to be, and may be advised against withdrawing a particular book, or asked to bring written approval from a parent. In several libraries there is either a place for, or a wish for, a staff member who has specialized in literature for the senior high school age group.

The tendency to differentiate between the younger and older adult reader undoubtedly reflects increased public anxiety about the rise in teenage delinquency. This has not increased alarmingly *in toto* perhaps, but youngsters from "good" middle class homes are more frequently reported than in the past. Parent, educator, and civic-minded citizen can no longer console themselves that when the slums are cleaned up delinquency will disappear. They begin to seek other explanations for the problems of this age group—including books in the public library. The librarians who discussed the pros and cons of a young people's collection were far more likely to stress its public relations value than they were to point to professional justifications.[3] The argument was sometimes heard that if you restrict the exposure of young people, more latitude will be possible in the adult collection.

DEVICES OF AFFIRMATION

We have seen that more questions about controversial books are raised by librarians themselves (or by school administrators and faculty members) than by individuals or groups in the community, and that patron or parental objections are resisted more often than are internal complaints (44 per cent resulted in restrictions or removals as compared with 85 per cent of the books complained about from within). About one-fourth of the librarians included in the study gave specific examples of an affirmative approach to public complaints, but most of them also cited other occasions on which they had capitulated to public

---

[3] The American Library Association encourages the development of young people's collections and the training of "young adult" specialists, but, again, its objectives in doing so are professional, not defensive.

pressures. It is difficult to detect any pattern in the complaints resisted and those which are not. A municipal librarian who retained
Burdick's *Ninth Wave* in the face of public complaint restricted Roark's
Something of Value. Another, who kept *Little Black Sambo*, withdrew a children's biography of Ralph Bunche. A school librarian who
defended the works of Louis Adamic withdrew *The Merchant of
Venice*. There is, however, sometimes a faint hint that the more solid
the work from the standpoint of factual accuracy, or literary worth
the more likely is it to be defended. Thus Steinbeck's *East of Eden*,
complained about on sex grounds, was defended by the same librarian
who restricted Lumbard's *Senior Spring* as a result of a similar complaint.

The methods of affirmation are, of course, not applied only to patron
or parental complaints about particular books. They may be applied
in the process of making selection decisions, or in a long-range, constructive program of education. Five more or less distinct methods,
each having a somewhat different psychological or intellectual basis,
are discernible: (1) the dramatic (rare); (2) the rational (the most
frequent but not necessarily the most successful); (3) the casual (infrequent, but highly successful under certain circumstances); (4) the
stand-up-and-be-counted (infrequent, but eminently successful in situations warranting forthright confrontation); and (5) the preventive
(rare but effective).

The dramatic approach.—For a few librarians, public threats (real
or imagined) to their institutions or to their professional autonomy are,
if not welcomed, at least utilized to put the library or the librarian in
the limelight. This may be just as true for a school librarian who
is one of many in a large city system as for a public librarian eager
to make himself felt within his community or his profession. Persons
who dramatize themselves, their professional roles, or their institutions
in this way take a strong stand where their competence or judgment
seems to be questioned or threatened, but not necessarily on less personal matters of principle. Among them are individuals who have
made public statements in support of intellectual freedom and the
freedom to read, but who, in private, exercise extreme caution in
selection or distribution. A school librarian, for example, who staunchly
and with great fanfare defended her collection against "women with
a list" in her library, is at the same time firmly convinced that books,
including many classics of English literature, can be harmful to young
people in a number of ways, and she reported in some detail how her
personal convictions influence her present selection for the school
library. A public librarian who vigorously and publicly defended the

presence of the Kinsey volumes in his library is a firm believer in "desk collections" and keeps many controversial books at the checkout desk instead of on the shelves because "otherwise we'd have a lot more trouble with a lot more books." Such people are certainly not publicity seekers, strictly speaking; nor, on the other hand, are they content to defend their judgments quietly. Attack or threat of attack becomes an opportunity for dramatization. They try to involve as many persons as possible in the situation. This is a self-centered (or at least self-interested) type of resistance to pressure. Although it accounts for comparatively few of the examples of confrontation reported in this study, a number of persons discussed situations which had occurred elsewhere in such a highly charged manner one suspects that if confronted with a complaint that lent itself to the purpose they, too, would utilize it for dramatic effect.

The rational approach.—The affirmative method that we have called "rational" is applicable both to complaints which the librarian receives from others and to material being considered for purchase which the librarian perceives as controversial. Persons utilizing and advocating this approach say that they resist complaints about books which they feel are "defensible," or that they would resist such complaints if the occasion were to arise. If, on the basis of their own judgment or on the basis of the judgment of other librarians or of reviewers they respect, a book appears to be "objective" or to have a claim to "esthetic validity," they are likely to purchase it and to defend its presence in the collection.

Thus, a book with sex content may be justified by a public librarian because "It was written with a purpose, was not pure sensationalism . . ." Similarly, a parent who complained that Irwin's *Young Bess* was too outspoken about the Queen's personal life was told that the facts were, if anything, understated and the book was kept in circulation. This is not to say librarians agree among themselves which books are defensible on such grounds. There are those who believe Steinbeck's *Grapes of Wrath* can be defended in a present-day collection but that its presence when it was most controversial in California was indefensible. There are others who hold opposite opinions just as warmly: "If I had been the librarian and the supervisors had told me to ban a book like that I would have resigned. I've never gotten over being ashamed for this library that we banned such a wonderful book." At least one (in this case a school librarian) has none of Steinbeck's works and would never buy anything by him because, she believes, he "distorts everything to fit in with the picture he wants to provide."

Actually, even firm grounds for affirmation may be worn down over time if the librarian is subjected to sustained outside pressure. To continue with Steinbeck as an example, a public branch librarian reported that:

> . . . when *Grapes of Wrath* first came out . . . people brought it back and said it was the filthiest thing they ever read. I tried to explain . . . that this was one phase of California life—that it had been accepted as truth by many people who lived in California. After a while you can no longer stand being faced with constant argument and then when the supervisor comes around you suggest . . . that perhaps some other branch ought to have the book for a while.

A more recent example of the wearing down effect of sustained pressure is found in a community with a newspaper which constantly badgers the schools and the libraries. Here the librarian's approach to complaints is usually rational, but she suspects that she may eventually be influenced by the campaign. "There's no reason on earth why anybody should give a second thought to buying Dorothy Canfield Fisher, yet because [the local newspaper] picked on her for a long time, the name does evoke a pang of doubt." While firmer and more consistent than the self-dramatizing approach, the rational may be subject to wear and tear.

The casual approach.—The casual approach also relates to the selection process as well as to actual complaints. Utilizing such an approach are the people who say, "We will have complaints as long as we have libraries. If we think we must avoid them, we might as well close up shop." Included among them are persons of philosophical bent: "Complaints go in cycles." "Most patron complaints should not be interpreted as pressures to ban a book." Others take an indulgent, non-reactive view: "People just like to talk about writers like Fast—I smile and let them talk." Only one person reporting habitual use of this approach has removed or restricted a book because of a complaint. Nor, apparently, have any objectors repeated a complaint or taken it to anyone else in the institution when confronted initially by such detachment. "These people who would complain about a book, I used to tell them, 'Well, you don't have to read it, you could just put the book aside if you didn't *really* want to read it.' That used to stop them cold."

The stand-up-and-be-counted approach.—This approach is, in the most literal sense, direct affirmation. The librarian who utilizes it is not defending his status or dramatizing his role, nor does he merely defend what he considers to be a defensible book nor simply let the patron talk himself out. The approach is used discriminatingly, and sometimes by persons who under most circumstances are much more casual. It is believed to be particularly applicable to persons who are extreme or dogmatic in their demands, or to persons whose main objective is to stir up dissension or to get publicity. It resembles the technique of fighting fire with fire: "If you stand right up to people like that, they quiet down." One premise from which this approach arises is that such complaints are not spontaneous but derivative: "Usually people get the idea to object from somewhere else, and when they can't make it stick here they give up pretty easily."

People who advocate a firm approach under such circumstances believe that the air is cleared if the overall function of the library is explained now and then. They also tend to feel that no great harm can come from restrictive campaigners *per se*, that even public conflicts may in the long run do good, because the librarian who thus confronts a complainant helps to clarify the principles of the profession, both for other professionals and for the public at large.

The majority of librarians have not been exposed to the kinds of complaints which warrant this assertive approach. But there are some who have been so exposed and who have given in to the complainant. One explanation for such capitulation may be that not enough attention is given to differentiating between various types of complaints and complainants. A librarian who has had good luck with the rational or the casual approach may simply adopt one of these as *the* method for dealing with all problems, treating the complainant who just wants to talk and the one who wants to conduct a campaign in exactly the same way. More important are two other factors: first, the sense of conflict between the professional and the public service role of the librarian; second, a special kind of mental facility is required to make such a confrontation in a telling fashion.

As to the sense of conflict, most public and school librarians (and school administrators as well) believe that the individuals or groups whose taxes help support a public institution have the right to complain about how it is run. They do not agree, however, as to what kinds of complaints, supported by how many and what kinds of people, should be permitted to influence library policy. There are school administrators, school librarians and school boards, public librarians, and library trustees who seem to believe that any individual or group who complains should not only be heard but heeded. Under these circumstances, almost every complaint results in a removal or a restriction. Such "democratic" policy in the long run circumscribes the whole collection. Much in the same way as the motion picture industry lost in substance by responding to all types of pressures (until tele-

vision siphoned most of them off), so may a library collection cease
to arouse the interest of all but the least demanding patrons by the
attempt to avoid complaints from all directions. As one city branch
librarian observed, sometimes there are not many complaints because
there is not much to complain about—no Blanshard because there are
many Catholics in the city, no Cela's *The Hive* because some people
construe things Spanish as "potentially Communist." As this librarian
and her colleagues pointed out, the system has a number of unsatisfied
patrons too, and even high school students in the city are more or less
officially advised to join a private library. Less extreme but more
numerous are those who react to a complaint one day and resist a
similar one the next, as though torn between concepts of democracy
and of professional functions which neither they nor their boards
have thought through and formulated for library policy. They are
typified by a person who was very articulate about her dislike of *Storm
Center*. Bette Davis was "too dictatorial"; the function of the librarian
in this day and age is not to educate but to "walk a tightrope."

The psychological obstacles to the stand-up-and-be-counted approach have been summed up by a librarian who is a veteran of
library-centered controversies. She spoke of how she thought crusaders
such as Mrs. X should be handled. She pointed out that a campaign
for censorship is most likely to be based on a particular book or books
or particular passages from them and that such a campaign is usually
highly emotional (or pseudo-rational). The defense, so far as a library
is concerned, is a defense of principle, not of particular books. It must,
therefore, be both general and rational. This means that when a book
is condemned the librarian must make a mental jump to a plane quite
different from that on which the objector is functioning. This is not,
for most people, a spontaneous affair. If someone says, "This book is
obscene," the immediate, unthinking response is likely to be, "It is
not," a reaction precisely on the level of, and in the same terms as,
the attack. According to this approach, whether it is or is not obscene
is not crucial.

Most librarians have pursued their careers in the light of some more
or less generalized concept of the function of a library in a free society.
It has been a half-formulated thought, for the most part, comfortably
stored away under the assumption that everyone else has more or less
the same idea. Suddenly, not a principle but a book is attacked, and
the habit of thought required to make the jump is simply not there.
To be sure, under the restrictive pressures of the post-war period some
librarians spontaneously made the jump or learned to make it. But
others remained trapped by the specificity of the objectors. It is diffi-

cult to defend a few quotations out of context, or a book or two (or fifteen) individually rather than as part of a collection. Where there have been many specific attacks over a relatively long period of time and the habit of making the jump has not been acquired, small wonder that a tangle of highly detailed and often contradictory "official" defenses has resulted.

The preventive approach.—Not many of the librarians who participated in this study have had the opportunity, or created an opportunity, to express their philosophy of book selection publicly. Those who have done so usually made their first pronouncements when under attack or when threatened with attack, and followed them up with additional public speeches or articles in professional journals. As they moved out from under the attack which precipitated their public statements, they became increasingly convinced that statements of principle may go far toward preventing future eruptions, providing that such pronouncements are compatible with their practices.

Whatever its effects on the public at large, there is evidence suggesting that the preventive or educational approach may have a marked effect on professionals who are in contact with others who utilize it. Within the study's sample were two large institutions whose chief executives have publicly—in writing and in speeches—defended the freedom to read against attacks of extremists. One of these two systems is democratically run and has selection policies which are consistent with public statements. The other tends toward autocratic leadership, and its policies are reactive to actual or potential community pressures. In the first institution, the majority of professionals consistently resist public pressures. In the second, where the executive has taken a dramatic public stand but where internal policies are inconsistent with it, staff members are cautious in their approach to book selection and capitulate to any and all complaints.

6

Paradox in School Librarianship

Considering the sharp difference in the structure of their organizations —school libraries are appendages, public libraries are institutions in themselves—the similarities between school and public librarians are striking. Their reactions to controversial materials follow the same pattern, so do their methods of resolution or compromise. Conflicts centering in school libraries have had major repercussions in public libraries, and pressures against public libraries have had critical impact on the policies and practices of school library systems. The presence of extremist groups in the community has an inhibiting effect on both school and public library practice. School as well as public librarians, if they work in large systems headed by restrictive administrators, tend to be restrictive in their own policies and practices, regardless of community pressures or lack of them. School librarians are, to be sure, more preoccupied with the controversial aspect of material for adolescents, but their ideas as to how this age group should be protected bear a notable resemblance to those of public librarians.

The most striking contrast between the two groups of professionals is that the personal characteristics which dispose public librarians to resist pressures do not have the same consequences for school librarians. The school librarians interviewed in this study were younger than the public librarians (table 3), and fewer than one-fourth of them have worked in librarianship for more than twenty years, compared with more than half of the public librarians (table 28). More of them have had professional training: 77 per cent of the school librarians have a librarianship degree or certificate, compared with 67 per cent of the county and 52 per cent of the municipal librarians (table 6). As we have seen, younger librarians and those with profes-sional training tend to resist pressures. But this is not the case among school librarians where we find more, rather than fewer, persons who habitually avoid the controversial. What then, are the forces at work upon school librarians which offset the effect of these usually stabiliz-ing characteristics?

In the reports of school librarians two themes are dominant: isola-tion and subordination—isolation both from the profession of librar-ianship and from faculty colleagues, and subordination to the con-cepts and practices of their school administrators. Furthermore, these states, or states of mind, are mutually reinforcing: the greater the sense of isolation the greater the subordination, and vice versa.

ISOLATION

About half the school librarians who were interviewed work in metro-politan areas where local and regional meetings of the two state library associations are regularly held. Yet a smaller proportion participate in such meetings than is the case among public librarians (table 29). (Membership in professional organizations, as distinguished from participation, is about the same for school as for public librarians, averaging around 80 per cent for each group—see table 34.) Lack of attendance at the annual meetings of the California Library Associa-tion (CLA), held in midweek, may be explained by the fact that, with the exception of one metropolitan system, no school librarians in our sample are given time off to attend professional conventions. The regional and state meetings of the School Library Association of Cali-fornia (SLAC) are held on weekends, however, and local and metro-politan area meetings of both organizations are usually held after school hours or on Saturdays.

The majority of school librarians belong to the California Teachers Association (CTA), but there is no evidence that activity in this organization accounts for the relative lack of interest in the profes-sional library groups. As a matter of fact, CTA membership, whether voluntary or enforced by the school administration, is usually nominal and is explained on grounds of material support. "After all, the CTA looks after our salary increases and things like that." (In most schools the salary scale of the librarian is the same as that of the teacher.) In short, the CTA is viewed as a kind of protective association rather than as an organization concerned with substantive professional prob-lems. There seems little reason why it should be otherwise. The or-ganization has no subdivision of school librarians, and apparently there has not been a conference program devoted to the school library for many years. The School Library Association of California is loosely affiliated with the CTA. It may be that CTA officers and committee chairmen assume that the less material interests of the school librarian are taken care of by that organization. The loose relationship between the two organizations was recently illustrated in the preparation of a CTA policy statement on controversial materials in the schools. In a preliminary draft of this document, to be distributed to school administrators and teachers throughout the state, the responsibilities and problems of school boards, administrators and teachers in regard to controversial materials were treated extensively. School libraries or librarians, often the chief targets of public controversy, were not mentioned at all. This draft was sent to the President of the School Library Association to distribute for comment among school library leaders. Needless to say, all noted the absence of discussion of the school library, and made constructive suggestions for library policy and practice. These comments were duly collated and forwarded to the CTA, but the final version remained uninfluenced by them.

CTA membership is expensive. A number of school librarians said that they could not afford to belong to both CTA and CLA. The dues of the School Library Association are more modest, but many school librarians believe that its benefits are modest as well. Some said that this organization is not energetic enough about looking after the interests of the profession by fighting censorship bills, for example, or in coming to the support of members who are threatened by restrictive measures in their schools or communities. (This attitude may well have changed somewhat as a result of SLAC's vigorous protest against the most recent book selection policy bill.) The association meetings are said to be devoted more to avoiding than to thinking through problems; as one member put it, "SLAC's programs are narrowing." Support for this viewpoint is found in the fact that proportionately more school librarians who are active in SLAC are restrictive in their own book selection practice than holds true for public librarians who are active in CLA.[1] School librarians, furthermore, read fewer professional journals (table 30); and among those who do read them the tendency to adopt a middle rather than a restrictive course is not so apparent as among public librarians.

The comparative isolation of school librarians from their colleagues is not compensated by community activity (table 31).[2] Some school

---

[1] Too few school librarians are active in CLA to determine whether it has a similarly "liberalizing" effect on them.

[2] Nor, apparently, is it accounted for by greater preoccupation with family responsibilities—in fact, proportionately fewer school than public librarians are married (table 5).

administrators discourage (or are said to discourage) community participation on the part of their faculties. In talking with school librarians, however, one does not get the impression that they feel thwarted by these unofficial regulations. In fact, neither isolation from the profession nor from the community seems to worry most of them. The estrangement of which most are aware is that experienced in their place of work. Nearly one-half of them indicated that other members of the faculty are indifferent to the library, that they did not feel welcome at departmental or curriculum meetings, or that no amount of effort and none of a variety of enticements arouses faculty coöperation in book selection. Only eight of the forty-five school librarians interviewed gave evidence of feeling well integrated with the faculty.

The most widely used technique for encouraging teacher participation in book selection is to not discourage it—that is, to buy anything requested. "I often order [teacher] request books even though I feel they're not suitable. Sometimes I *know* there's something better . . . but more rigorous screening would discourage what little interest teachers do have in book selection." Acceding to faculty requests is also viewed as a way of enhancing the school library's public relations: "If I buy what they want, then they feel committed to using the library for their classes." Eighteen of our school librarians utilize this approach. Fourteen go even farther and systematically attempt to elicit faculty participation. They send out order cards periodically; they route reviews and distribute check-off lists. They do this despite the feeling that by and large the results of such efforts are negligible. All in all, the amount of teacher-initiated buying is, if one holds it desirable, not encouraging. "Very little" or, "Oh, less than 10 per cent" is a common estimate of the proportion of books suggested by faculty. One librarian estimated 60 per cent, another 50 per cent, but the average is only slightly more than 20 per cent, and the median only half that.

Not all efforts to elicit faculty coöperation are completely wholehearted, however. Several—among whom are those with the most complaints against professional isolation—are so possessive about their libraries, and require so many details for a faculty order, that it would be surprising if any amount of encouragement were effective. The school librarian, considerably more than the public librarian, distinguishes between requests and "objective needs." It is evident that many who accede to faculty suggestions believe they are compromising their professional competence in doing so. "I'm always very careful to screen [teacher-selected books]. . . . Teachers are . . . enthusiastic one day and then tomorrow they forget all about the book. . . . So

I have to be sure the book has enduring value." Or, "The teacher who recommends buying a book must be willing to accept responsibility for the choice." As the latter observation suggests, the problem in regard to faculty requests is not always whether the book has intrinsic worth, but whether it might contain controversial materials. "Teachers," as another school librarian said, "tend to order things which are too mature." The insistence on "responsibility" is strongest in the larger systems where orders are screened in the superintendent's office. Order cards, under these circumstances, may call for a teacher's as well as a librarian's signature. One librarian hinted at the necessity for forgery, since teachers are not always willing to assume such responsibility.

Aside from the general indifference (or caution) attributed to administration and faculty, the lament most frequently heard is, "The teachers think we librarians have nothing to do." School librarians complain more about being overworked than do public librarians, but it is usually clear that they are comparing their work schedules not with those of public librarians but with teachers. In order to provide students with access to the library outside of class hours, librarians generally arrive at school earlier and leave later than the rest of the faculty. Furthermore, some school librarians work at the beginning or the end of summer vacation, when the rest of the faculty does not. Several take lunch at a different time than the rest of the faculty in order to keep the library open for students when classes are not in session. A few have no relief and take only fifteen or twenty minutes for lunch, sometimes in the library workroom or office. A number of school librarians who are free for the regular lunch hour eat with the school nurse or with their assistants or clerks rather than with the faculty.

Of the nineteen school librarians who discussed the allocation of their work time in any detail, eleven regularly take work home with them, or come back to school on Saturday in order to do their book selection. Several also prepare for and attend book review sessions on their own time. Only one school librarian reported that she always "leaves the job at school," while nine public librarians made this point. (Of thirty public librarians discussing time use, only seven indicate regular homework or overtime for book selection.)

Responsibility for ordering, processing, and distributing textbooks is the task which most librarians believe makes their work load excessive. More than half have this responsibility, although clerks or junior librarians usually assist them (table 32). But even with assistance, very few find it natural that this processing should be the responsibility of the librarian. Most consider it undignified and out of keeping with their professional status, the more so, no doubt, since they are rarely members of a school's textbook committee. Taking care of texts, which requires large amounts of manual and clerical activity, is offered as one explanation for the feeling that "the faculty and students think we are just clerks." Study hall and the supervision of disciplinary cases (or "atypicals," as the current terminology in some schools has it) are other tasks generally viewed as interferences with the proper functions of a librarian (notably book selection). Here, too, the resentment is not about the extra chore or even its drain on time and energy, but about its implied depreciation of professional status. One librarian whose principal told her of his plan to institute a library study hall for students whose " 'ambition is just a little higher than their abilities' " was enthusiastic about this "challenge to . . . ingenuity." When she found that all but two of her thirty-five study hall pupils were "just plain deadwood that has to be shoved someplace to fill out their time," her interest was dampened a little. Teachers, the school librarians believe, have learned how to protect themselves. As one respondent put it, teachers in California "have so long and so loudly proclaimed that civilization depends on them that they've become convinced of it themselves. Administrators are very cautious about asking a teacher to take on some extra chore."

About one-third of our school librarians teach a "library science" class, and this task is viewed as quite in keeping with their professional duties. The majority are impressed, however, with the lack of appeal of librarianship for students; this together with their extra-professional duties adds a feeling of inferiority to that of isolation. Nearly every one of the seventeen school librarians who are former teachers believes that she has lost status as a result of the change, despite having added a library credential to her teaching credential, usually with concomitant salary increments.

The school librarian, then, does not often feel physically or intellectually integrated with the faculty, and reacts to what is construed as faculty underestimation of the librarian's function by complaining about being overworked. When comparing themselves with public library colleagues, another type of defensiveness sometimes appears. The fact is—and it has been duly noted by public librarians—that the beginning librarian is likely to be offered a substantially higher salary in a school than in a public library (although in the limited upper echelons, the salary range in public librarianship is higher). Consequently a number of our school librarians have tortured themselves with questions about their motives—a practice which may be stimulated at the professional schools where, it has been said, the career choices of school librarians are sometimes deprecated as materialistic or escapist. In any event, while there is no evidence to support the view that school librarians are less dedicated to their work than public librarians, there is ample evidence that they are more defensive about their career choice. In some interviews it was almost as though the respondent assumed an unspoken question: "Why are you a *school* librarian?" One or two, as if ruminating on this imagined question, spoke of the "dangers" of tenure and retirement pay, quite forgetting that the majority of public librarians now fall under civil service and have as much security as school librarians. (The head municipal librarian, however, usually serves "at the pleasure of the board," and the head county librarian is normally appointed for a four year term.) Those school librarians who are former teachers were no more defensive than the rest, despite the fact that it is sometimes said (by an official of CTA, for example, as well as by school administrators) that school librarians who have taught in the past were probably encouraged by their principals to make the change because they were judged to be incompetent in the classroom. Actually, most of the former teachers were not apologetic; they were clear and forthright in stating their reasons for making the change—often on grounds of finding the present content and methods of teaching incompatible with their personal ideals of education. Many believed they could influence students' creative and intellectual development much more effectively as librarians. Furthermore, although a high proportion of school librarians who have not taught have credentials for teaching, not one of them expressed a wish to change from the library to the classroom.

This sense of incompatibility with the methods and content of contemporary public education was not limited to those librarians who had been teachers. Throughout the interviews, regardless of the age of the respondent, runs a strong undercurrent of perplexity and dismay.

Take the emphasis in the school programs here— It's California, California, California. . . . There is, of course, local discretion, but on the whole the emphasis is on California—its history, its accomplishments, its future. It is . . . fantastically disproportionate to the State's importance in the nation or in the world and history.

According to another, "There's no leadership to promote library-centered pedagogy, and it's a pity because the best way to reach the adolescent is through books." The practice of passing every student, or of "social promotion" by whatever name, results in an influx into the senior high school of students whose reading level may be only that of a second- or third-grader. So much money and energy has to be devoted to the difficult task of finding material that combines senior high school interests with elementary school reading level that little time is left to devote to the "good" readers.

Moreover, the increase in curriculum coördinators and supervisors at various levels (in individual schools, municipal systems, county systems and in the State Department of Education) means more memoranda and more meetings for teachers and less time for students. Several school librarians thought that this money could provide more personnel at the operating level—in the classrooms and libraries—with immeasurably more constructive results. The emphasis on procedure (the "organization mania," as one librarian called it) and on interpersonal relations distracts teacher and student alike from content. Caution about controversial books on the part of both teacher and administrator results in more and more avoidance of the library. The comment that "even the English teachers haven't read a book since they left college" may exaggerate somewhat, but typifies the rather widespread conviction that books, even in the schools, do not receive as much respect as they used to.

School librarians, then, although they work in institutions where there are many more colleagues of comparable professional status than does the public librarian, feel—and often are—isolated. In part, this situation may be explained by the comparative youth of the profession of school librarianship and the fact that, because of its relationship to the larger institutions of public education, it did not start off fully integrated with the field of librarianship as a whole. All the problems and insecurities common to the profession at large are enhanced by a sense of inferiority to it. School librarians feel like second-class members of their own profession and like second-class members of their own faculties. More activity or status in the former might provide the impetus for attaining status in the latter. At present, these two uncertainties seem to reinforce each other, with the result that school librarians become highly susceptible to the influence of their administrators.

SUBORDINATION

School administrators and teachers are, by and large, trained in schools of education. School librarians are usually trained in schools of librarionship. In neither training center, apparently, is much attention paid to exploring and defining the role of the school library in the educational process. Nor is there any evidence that the function of the school library is a matter of concern at the state level. There is a visual aids division but no library division in the State Department of Education; and if a library consultant is ever provided, librarians are likely to find it difficult to avoid having this post subordinated to that of the visual aids expert. The optimistic librarian says, "We need a school library consultant on the state level because we have no one to turn to." The pessimist (or realist) says, "We are not known as libraries any more, we are 'instructional materials centers,'" and points out that budgets for film, records, recorders, and projectors are leaping upward at the expense of books and periodicals. Like the California Teachers Association, the State Department of Education collects no special information about libraries or librarians on a regular or systematic basis.[3] Plans for new schools are approved by a committee of architects for the Department of Education, but it is apparently a matter of local wisdom or whim whether the blueprints include libraries and whether their layouts are adequate for their function. That most senior high schools now being built have libraries is a consequence of the accreditation requirement of the Board of Regents of the University of California. In some overcrowded schools, even new ones, libraries have been appropriated as classrooms for much of the school day. One library included in this study is maintained in the cafeteria, where it competes not only with sandwiches and soda but with a juke box. In three of the schools visited, library appropriations had recently been cut in order to help support an increase in teacher salaries.

Such handicaps notwithstanding, about one-third of our school librarians have what might be called a vigorously positive approach to the function of the school library. They dwelt long and enthusiastically on the importance of developing a love of reading and an appreciation of books. "Books . . . record the wisdom and follies of man, and in its broadest interpretation the object of education is to transmit knowledge and understanding of both . . ." "Provoking thought should, behind all its other functions, be the basic aim of a school library." Approximately another third of the school librarians are mainly preoccupied with the more routine aspects of their work (processing, discipline, controversiality, mutilation and stealing of

---

[3] The State Library collects basic data, annually, about school as well as county and municipal libraries. Contributing to such information is, on the part of the schools, a voluntary matter, and school library information tends (judging from our sample of schools, at least) to be somewhat spotty or obsolete. The resource most relied upon by all agencies is Mary McWilliam's "A Survey of Library Resources in the California Public High Schools" (doctoral dissertation, University of California, 1956) which was undertaken with the encouragement and coöperation of both the California State Library and the California State Department of Education.

books, and the like). They spoke of problem books and lamented faculty, administrative and community disinterest. They seldom mentioned students, and when they did it was to deplore book thieves or the many low-level readers for whom material cannot be found. Among these rather negatively oriented school librarians are three who complained at great length about the necessity to "read, read, and read" because the standard fiction reviews do not take into account the special problems (by which they meant sex and crude language) of the high school librarian. There were also four who feel justified in avoiding fiction altogether—at least modern fiction—on the grounds that "it's safer for us if they get their novels somewhere else," or, in a more rationalistic vein, because "the school library must not compete with the public library."

The remaining third of our school librarians are neither very hopeful nor very discouraged. They speak of library objectives briefly, using general phrases such as "to supplement the curriculum and to provide enrichment reading," or ask, "Can't I just go along with whatever the ALA [or CLA or SLAC] has to say on that?" But a few in this apparently noncommittal group are more interested in the library's role than they cared to admit. They hinted that headquarters, the administration, or the curriculum itself, prevents them from developing their libraries as fully and freely as they would like. Some go along, but ruefully: "We have to tie [each book selected] to 'education'. . . . I just write in some standard clichés I've got in the habit of using." Others criticize these pat formulas: "There is really no split between 'curriculum supplementation' and 'just reading.' There just appears to be a split because the curriculum is not well-rounded." Or, "We cannot integrate [the library] with the curriculum because there is no curriculum to integrate with."

School administrators' concepts of the function of the library are not quite so readily gauged. About one-third of those visited were so involved with other matters [4] or so unwilling to be interviewed that it was impossible to determine their opinions at all, except insofar as the avoidance of the interview is indicative. Prior to the interviewer's arrival, all school superintendents in the districts covered were sent letters describing the study's auspices, objectives and advisory committee (which included the then President of the California Association of School Administrators and a well-known member of the faculty

---

[4] At the time of the field work, three of the twenty-nine districts were in the midst of upheaval at the board or administrative level; three had undergone severe shakeouts within the preceding year; and in another six, superintendents had obtained their posts following a radical overturn earlier.

of the School of Education at the University of California). The interviewer's usual procedure was to telephone and if possible to visit the superintendent first. The superintendent, or a delegated associate, was again told the purpose and procedures of the study and invited to discuss the functions of the school library (especially those in his system) and to review the numbers and types of schools to be visited locally. Eleven superintendents, two persons who held the combined office of superintendent and principal, twenty-five principals or vice-principals and ten supervisors of curriculum or instructional directors (office of superintendent) were visited.

Three principals were openly hostile and accused the interviewer of "snooping." It became apparent later that their librarians had been briefed to say as little as possible, or to find some pretext for cutting the interview short. In two of these three instances both principals and librarians avoided mentioning rather well-known episodes about controversial books which had taken place in their schools within the past two years. One principal remarked, "You're going to be disappointed here, we've had no trouble at all." With a few exceptions, superintendents and principals who had had previous experience in teaching academic subjects showed an interest in their libraries; those who were former coaches, physical education or shop teachers were relatively indifferent. Among those for whom we have no background information, more had a favorable orientation toward the library than a negative one. Even administrators who were interested and coöperative in regard to the study occasionally refused to provide background information about themselves (interviewers were instructed not to press the point). But since training and former professional experience of the administrator seem to have some bearing on his attitude toward the library, it is perhaps relevant to repeat here that for those about whom background information could be procured, nine were former coaches or physical education or shop teachers; one was a former drama coach; three had specialized in business administration or taught business courses; four had taught social studies courses, and five had taught unspecified subject matter.

School administrators' concepts of the function of the school library are even more wide-ranging than those of the librarians. When negative, they are a great deal more so: "All we need is a self-help machine," or "If the library isn't used for a classroom, what good is it?" Those who were positive, on the other hand, were likely to view the library as the center of the school, as a coördinating and centralizing force counterbalancing what one construed as the fact that "the high school curriculum is doomed to fragmentation." Even this man, however, exerted his influence only indirectly, and was relatively out of touch with his school's librarian.

Altogether, there are more administrators with a creative and positive approach to the library (twelve out of the twenty-five who were willing to discuss the matter) than there are with sharply negative opinions (four). The rest are either indifferent or so preoccupied with other matters that they have neither time nor energy for consideration of the library's role. The orientation of the faculty toward the school library can be viewed here only through the eyes of administrators and librarians. The main impression (and library-oriented administrators agree with their librarians on this) is that, aside from an occasional English or social studies teacher, teachers do not encourage their students to embark on unsupervised explorations of the library. Some librarians believe there is not only indifference but avoidance in their faculties, as if from anxiety.

For nineteen schools, we are able to pair off principals and librarians and to compare the principal's attitudes toward the library with the librarian's feeling of integration or lack of it. Eight of the nineteen principals are clearly library-oriented. In all but one instance their respective librarians have good working relationships with the faculty, feel welcome at departmental meetings, and believe the staff to be relatively coöperative about book selection. In the other eleven schools, administrators manifest indifference to the library, and ten of them have librarians who feel isolated. Typical comments from librarians in these schools were, "each teacher goes his own way," "they all think I'm just a clerk," "I feel cut off, somehow," or, "nothing I've tried gets [the faculty's] interest or coöperation, and, what's more, the teachers think I just sit here and read all day." Occasionally these expressions of dissatisfaction are directed toward the principal who is, explicitly or implicitly, likely to be held responsible for this state of affairs.

The principal is a former sports coach, and the only things you can really arouse him about are the sports programs. . . . He means well, no doubt, but has no conception of what goes into making a library run. . . . In some ways, I suppose it's just as well if the principal stays out of library affairs when it's that sort of man—but it would be nice to feel that your efforts are appreciated and sympathized with.

Administrators who are indifferent toward the library tend to be restrictive in their philosophies of book selection and, conversely, those who are library-oriented tend to be free of such constraints. But, while the principal's general attitude toward the library has a strong bearing on the librarian's sense of isolation, it has little or no effect on the librarian's restrictiveness. Restrictive librarians were found with library-oriented principals, and nonrestrictive librarians had principals who were indifferent to the library.

The relationship between the principal's attitude toward controversiality and his librarian's attitude toward book selection and distribution is nearly as remarkable as the connection between his general orientation to the library and the librarian's sense of isolation. Of the fourteen principals who have a restrictive or cautious orientation, eleven have librarians who are also clearly restrictive. Of the fourteen principals who expressed strong "freedom to read" concepts, ten have librarians who are not restrictive in their practices.

The relationship between the attitudes of superintendents and of principals (or between superintendents and librarians, for that matter) cannot be traced clearly because of the comparatively small number of superintendents interviewed. Superintendents were freer in their orientation to controversial materials than were principals—but permissive superintendents are just as likely to have cautious or restrictive principals in their systems as are the more restrictive superintendents, or a restrictive superintendent may have a nonrestrictive principal.

In two of the systems having library coördinators, the views and behavior of the librarians more closely resemble those of the library supervisor than those of the principal in whose schools they happen to work. One of the smaller coördinated systems has a highly restrictive supervisor and here a principal-librarian team frequently joins forces in an attempt to liberalize the policy. In one of the large systems, the superintendent delegated the interview to the library supervisor and it seemed to be assumed by all concerned that principals should not be bothered with library problems. (Only one school librarian interviewed in this system even mentioned a principal, in any context, but she and all of her colleagues repeatedly referred to their supervisor.)

Having painted this picture of isolation and dependence, it is important to recall that, while there are more school than public librarians who are consistently restrictive, there are also more school librarians who are not restrictive at all (table 14). No doubt much of this tendency to cluster at either end of the continuum results from the reinforcement provided by the principal's leadership in one direction or the other. But there are also a few librarians who are not restrictive in spite of strong restrictiveness on the part of their principals. Some have tried, with varying degrees of success, to reason matters out and to liberalize formal or informal policy. Others simply act in a less cautious manner than their principals believe them to act (which may account for the fact that, unlike public librarians, school librarians are sometimes freer in deed than their words would indicate). But neither they nor the leaders in the profession of school librarianship harbor much hope that the equivocal position of the school library and the school librarian can be changed on an individual basis. As one of our respondents said, school libraries "are neither fish nor fowl." Neither school librarians nor school administrators (even were they so inclined) can determine function or policy separately, and so far as we have been able to determine, neither in training institutions, in professional organizations nor in the public schools themselves have these two groups met to explore the problem jointly. Administrators, as one library supervisor remarked, are both "out of touch and out of reach."

7

THE PROFESSIONAL IMAGE

In examining the treatment of controversial materials in public and high school libraries, it was also necessary to inspect the librarian's environment; the general tenets and practices of book selection had to be equated with the community and institutional settings. Throughout this examination we have glimpsed now and then more personal factors which also bear on the treatment of the controversial. We need much more information about the subjective experiences of librarians than is available in this study to understand fully the role of the professional self-image whose subtleties were hinted during the interviews. What follows is largely impressionistic, a culling of librarians' concepts of their advantages and disadvantages as professionals. For the most part, it was through discussions of their training schools and professional organizations that this image became clear. But first a word about the "state."

THE STATE

In view of the insecurities of public librarians and school administrators in relation to their communities, and of school librarians in relation to their schools, it would come as no surprise if they looked to state institutions, such as the State Library or the Department of Education, for support. Actually, while school librarians do harbor some expectations in this direction, the commonest attitude toward state agencies is one of detachment, or indifference, occasionally of fear.

The school principal who said, "We public school educators are instruments of the state," may or may not have meant the state of

California. If he did, he would probably find very few colleagues who would agree with him. Most of the school administrators who participated in this study looked upon anything emanating from "the state" as a threat. Bills, measures or directives issuing from the Legislature or the State Department of Education are distrusted. Administrators see tentacles reaching out through the offices of the county superintendents of schools to threaten local autonomy. They can conceive no other explanation for the Department's and superintendencies' ever-expanding networks of supervisors, specialists and coördinators than a desire to build up a political machine. What they believe the objectives of this machine to be, beyond self-perpetuation and expansion, they did not make clear. Except in rural areas, the county superintendent's office is thought to be superfluous.

School librarians, on the other hand, cast hopeful eyes toward the state level. Unlike their administrators, who feel that the less the state has to do with any aspect of local education the better, school librarians seem to feel that many of their problems will be solved by the establishment of a library supervisor or library consultant in the Department of Education. A number of public librarians and members of the staff of the State Library [1] also believe that the establishment of such a post would be a good thing for the profession in general and for the school librarian in particular. In fact, some members of the State Library staff, and a few other library leaders in the state, advised their colleagues not to oppose a bill making it mandatory for school boards to establish and control library policy. They maintained that a struggle on this issue would antagonize the legislature and jeopardize the long-pending bill for the establishment of the post of library consultant (as well as a bill for a statewide survey of library resources). The School Library Association of California officially opposed the policy bill, while the California Library Association, which was originally against it, ceased to fight a diluted version. [2] (As we have already noted, the policy bill was pocket-vetoed by the Governor; the bill establishing the post of library consultant again was not passed.)

Although the State Library is at the apex of the county systems,

---

[1] The State Library, although technically a division in the Department of Education, has no official relationship to school librarians.

[2] This was the bill initiated by Mrs. X in 1955 and reintroduced in 1957 (see chap. 5, p. 55). The second bill was eventually watered down, stating that school library policy should be established by the school board but not enumerating (as had the first bill, by reference to part of the state education code) what kind of material would or would not be permitted. Some librarians believed that no censorship issues were involved in the new version.

county librarians are relatively unconcerned with its actual or potential influence on their policies. The State Library promotes standards for personnel and services, provides administrative and technical assistance to county and municipal systems of all sizes and types, and maintains an extensive book and periodical service on interlibrary loan. Both municipal and county librarians went out of their way to praise the completeness and efficiency of the book and periodical services, but it was librarians in the smaller municipal libraries who expressed the most appreciation for its consultative functions.

Municipal librarians, while grateful for the resources and services of the State Library, showed signs of anxiety about its potential influence. As the field work of the study progressed, a bill providing for a statewide survey of library resources and needs moved through the Legislature, and the interviewers began to note expressions of concern resembling those of the school administrators vis-à-vis the Department of Education. Some municipal librarians believed that the survey might be an attempt from the state level, by which they meant mainly the State Library, to exert control over municipal libraries. This fear had its basis in the assumption that State Library personnel favor an amalgamation of county and municipal systems in many areas (an amalgamation vigorously opposed by most municipal librarians).[3]

By and large, it is to their professional organizations and schools rather than to state agencies that librarians look for enhancement of their professional image and support of their professional role. These reinforcements are what the majority feels are essential to the more effective resistance of restrictive pressures.

PROFESSIONAL ORGANIZATIONS

Most professional organizations go through a series of typical phases in the course of their development. In the beginning, before a group has acquired publicly acknowledged professional status, its organizations have mainly social and inspirational functions. A great deal of time, during this phase, is devoted to soul searching. Whether the group does comprise a profession is the foremost question. If public acknowledgment or demand for the services of its members grows, the group tries to consolidate its membership. It debates qualifications for admission to the profession and may attempt to raise and to standardize status and salary levels. As the organization grows in numbers

[3] This bill was subsequently passed, and a citizens' advisory committee, including four members of the Legislature, was established. Known as the California Public Library Commission, this group, early in 1958, appointed Professor Edward A. Wight of the School of Librarianship, University of California, Berkeley, to direct the survey.

and influence, it establishes measures to protect its members from outside encroachments, from other professions or would-be professions, or from "quacks." Only when such consolidation is well under way is the professional association likely to concentrate on the more substantive aspects of its field.

Adult education, for example, now comprises a highly diversified group of activities, knowledge and skills, and might be said to be in the first phase, with much time devoted to whether adult education is or should be a well-defined professional field. Teachers' associations in many states are in the second phase, with the memberships devoted to raising salary levels and to enhancing the public image of the profession. Psychologists are a good example of professionals so much in public demand that they feel they must protect the public and themselves against quacks. Medical associations and academic disciplines in the natural sciences are professional groups which have attained sufficient inner security and public recognition to be able to devote much of their attention to scientific problems.

For librarianship, there seems little doubt that, on the national level, the profession has solved enough of its status and credential problems to be able to devote itself to substantive matters and to keeping an eye out for threats against the traditional freedoms of librarians and their publics. State, county and municipal associations of librarians, on the other hand, differ widely in their major preoccupations. These differences seem to be related to the degree of urbanization of the area they serve, to the proportion of members who are professionally trained, and to the age of the organizations. Two-thirds of the school librarians in our sample belong to the School Library Association of California (SLAC), almost half of them belong to the California Library Association (CLA), and one-quarter belong to the American Library Association (ALA). More than three-fourths of the municipal and county librarians belong to the California Library Association, and almost half belong to ALA. Nearly twice the proportion of public as school librarians belong to the national organization (table 34). Membership in the ALA (or in the national association of school librarians) is not automatically acquired with membership in the state groups, and several public librarians who formerly worked in other parts of the country dropped their national affiliations upon moving west, because ALA was "too far away."

The majority of our respondents felt that all librarians who work in a professional capacity [4] should belong to a professional organization

_____
[4] The California State Library defines the professional librarian as follows: "Professional employees are defined as those who are college or university and library

(all but fifteen do), but their reasons for holding this belief varied widely. Older librarians often say that they attend professional meetings to see friends and for "fellowship," others feel that professional memberships enhance their local prestige. This endorsement of the importance of professional memberships notwithstanding, there are signs both of indifference and of dissatisfaction. About a dozen of our respondents, mainly school librarians, were uncertain whether they belonged to SLAC or CLA, whether they served on any committees, or which ones. The majority of both school and public librarians, even those who are or have been officers or on committees, refer to their organizations as "they," complaining in the manner of an employee in a large bureaucracy that members are not kept informed, are not duly consulted, and that a clique of executives from large systems is in power. Local and regional affiliates of the state organizations, particularly those consisting of library executives or of children's librarians, are less often viewed in this negative light. They are "our" organizations and "we" decide what issues warrant discussion and action.

Altogether, the librarians who discussed the role of professional organizations had more negative than positive things to say about them. Most common was the complaint that the two state groups (CLA and SLAC) do not come to grips with controversial issues either on the local or the state level. Members do not feel that they will be backed up by the profession in the event of a local controversy. There were several complaints about the lack of a forthright stand on oath controversies and UN-UNESCO conflicts. A few went on to observe that, in the face of the threats of several censorship bills in the 1957 Legislature, the state organizations had "rallied a bit."

Next in importance to the complaints that the state organizations do not fight aggressively enough on matters of intellectual freedom are observations that they have not faced up to the important role and status problems of the profession. Members are convinced that the two state organizations could do more to dramatize the library and to enhance the public image of the librarian. They realize that programs of this sort require money; but a number of them feel strongly enough on this point to be willing to pay higher dues providing the money is used to fight censorship and to develop a program of public education. Among activities suggested for such a program were the establishment of a statewide speakers' bureau offering talks on such subjects as intellectual freedom, and the role of the school or

---

school graduates, and employees who have attained professional status through library experience and/or examination. They perform work of professional grade which requires training and skill in the theoretical or scientific parts of library work . . ." *News Notes of California Libraries*, LII: 1 (January, 1957), 24.

public library in the community, the maintenance of a lobbyist in the state capitol, and the development of closer relations with other state professional organizations.

It is recognized, however, that the professional organizations are in transition. They may not be able to concentrate on such problems until all librarians working in a professional capacity have professional training. But it was pointed out that library leaders act as individuals as well as association officers. For the time being, perhaps, their individual initiative offers the greatest possibility for strengthening the public and self-image of the profession. This might be an effective approach, for example, in countering restrictive pressures and upholding the freedom to read. Persons who are leaders on the national, state or regional level are less restrictive in their book selection behavior than those who are not. (Those library leaders whose influence on their colleagues is confined to the local level, curiously enough, are more restrictive than state and regional leaders. They are also more restrictive than those who have no influence on their colleagues at all —see table 35.) If they become more assertive as individuals, it is assumed that they would provide both practical and moral support to those members who have strong beliefs but are unable, or are thwarted in their efforts, to express them locally. On the few occasions when leaders of the profession have taken a strong and open stand on controversial issues, many librarians throughout the state have silently applauded, and felt strengthened in dealing with their own problems.

PROFESSIONAL SCHOOLS

It is within the framework of such problems as enhancing the public image of the librarian and encouraging a more positive public evaluation of the library that the conflict over "professionalism" becomes most intense. Those who believe that eventually all librarians should be professionally trained assume that the realization of this goal will take care of such problems as public image and community status. But opinion about the necessity of professional training is by no means unanimous. In the national organizations and in the leading schools of librarianship where a most vigorous defense of professional standards is maintained, there are lively and forthright discussions which face the fact that the librarian of today performs many functions for which professional education need not be required. The question has been raised whether new categories of non-professionals and technicians should not be devised.[5]

Sixteen public librarians in this study spontaneously observed that

---

[5] See Edward A. Wight, "Implications for Personnel," *The Library Quarterly*, XXVII: 4 (October, 1957), 305–319.

they do not believe professional training is a necessary prerequisite for carrying out what are considered to be professional responsibilities. The majority of the persons who hold this belief have themselves had graduate training in librarianship and several are heads of sizable institutions or leaders in the state organization. For the most part, these sixteen persons believe that a well-educated and well-rounded person can be trained on the job for almost any library activity. School librarians seem to hold a different opinion. Despite the fact that during the period of the field work for this study at least one leader in school librarianship was working actively to have the requirements for the certification of school librarians lowered, no school librarian expressed the belief that professional training could be supplanted by on-the-job training. This is in part a reflection of the situation in which the school librarian works. Except in one metropolitan system, the majority of even the largest senior high schools have only one librarian, making on-the-job training a virtual impossibility.

The supporters of complete professionalization face many inconsistencies. All except the smallest of the public libraries visited (and one large system having a very small percentage of employees with formal library training), bar personnel who are not designated as professionals from participation in book selection. It is the nonprofessionals, however, who have the most contact with clients. And the majority of our respondents have stressed the importance of client contact for effective book selection. Branch personnel are generally without formal professional training. Yet, within the limitations of what is purchased and sent out from headquarters, they have complete control over their collections. Despite the widespread opinion favoring on-the-job training, lectures or discussion programs are rarely provided for branch heads. In two systems where they attend "evaluation sessions," book selection principles are not discussed, nor are the branch heads asked to describe or evaluate the interests and needs of their communities. The purpose of these meetings, as described by headquarters librarians, is to familiarize branch personnel with the new books which have already been selected for the system.

Interviewers' questions about degree-granting training institutions focused on library philosophy, book-selection policy, and attitudes toward the controversial, but some forty of our respondents launched into a broader discussion of their schools. Their observations were predominantly critical, and three problems arose most frequently: the advanced degree, recruitment, and the content and tone of the curriculum.

In its 1951 "Standard for Accreditation," the ALA substituted the

Master of Science in Librarianship for the Bachelor of Library Science or certificate in librarianship formerly awarded to one-year graduate students. By August, 1957, all twenty-nine accredited United States Schools were granting the higher degree. The general programs required do not differ markedly from those formerly given for the certificate or the B.L.S., and some schools have issued official statements verifying the equivalence of their former certificate or B.L.S. with the newer M.L.S. Many respondents who graduated from library school before the advanced degree was granted feel that they worked just as hard for the certificate or B.L.S. as present graduates do for a master's degree. Several public librarians holding a certificate or B.L.S. have seriously thought of returning to school for the advanced degree because they believe the M.L.S. elicits higher status. Whether this belief stems from a conviction about the importance of degrees or from some actual financial or status advantage of the recent graduates is not clear from our material. What is clear is that most persons who considered returning to school decided against it, on the grounds that "unreasonable" amounts of additional course credits were required.

Among school librarians, the situation is more complex. Some say that had they the higher degree they would be farther along in their school systems' pay scale, while others believe it would make no difference. This uncertainty may have been connected with the concurrent discussions about lowering the requirements for state certification in school librarianship. It may also reflect factual differences in school policies, or a lack of clarity in them.

The shortage of trained librarians throughout the state—in both public and school libraries—was frequently attributed to recruitment shortcomings at the training centers. Indeed, this criticism was more common than seems warranted by the steady increase of enrollment in California. High school students, critics observed, know little about the profession—its requirements, its challenges, and its job opportunities; nor do they know that salary levels have risen in recent years. The belief is widespread that most of the accredited library schools select students who are particularly interested in university, college, and special library work, with the result that a withdrawn or "egghead" stereotype is reinforced which in turn frightens away students who might otherwise be attracted to public librarianship. Several respondents noted that the basic pool for library personnel is the same as that which supplies teachers, and then pointed to the forceful campaign which has stirred up that pool in behalf of teacher recruitment. Through the efforts of their professional organizations, through PTA's and the mass media, teaching is beginning to acquire the aura of a "civic service crusade" and the teacher the halo of a near-saint. Schools of education, they pointed out, engage very actively in the recruitment of students, sending brochures and speakers to high schools and undergraduate colleges. Neither the professional organizations nor the training centers of librarianship, these respondents feel, have made the most of such possibilities.

People who discussed the certificate-degree problem usually were talking about a personal grievance; those who mentioned recruitment by the professional schools were, for the most part, executives with recruitment problems of their own. The discussions of curriculum tone and content were, on the other hand, both less subjective and more intense. While the emphasis of these observations varied, one theme prevailed: professional education, by placing too much emphasis on details, leaves the student unprepared for the impact of the job situation in which he later finds himself. (Here, perhaps, we should remember that this is a criticism voiced by public and public school librarians; college, university and special librarians might have a different view.)

This theme was played in a number of keys. A few persons felt that library schools do not provide enough intellectual ferment. They look upon their institutions not as mere instruments of public service but as dynamic organs of individual and social development. They believe that this concept of the library can be encouraged only if the "cause" of librarianship is stressed over and above the learning of skills and techniques. The training offered today, said one young woman, "does not liberalize, it constricts," leaving the librarian more susceptible to what she called the "myths of the community."

A more specific grievance was that the basic tenets of librarianship are passed over too lightly in library school courses. Often as a consequence of recognizing inconsistencies in the concepts they themselves drew upon in the course of the interviews, respondents would stop short, asking themselves, in effect: What *am* I talking about? Balance, standards, public need, community responsibilities, well-rounded collection—what do they all mean? These are among the fundamental premises of librarianship, yet many respondents suddenly realized, at some point in the interview, that they have never explored their often diverse meanings and implications. Half a dozen explicitly accused the training centers of nurturing ambiguities and jargon and of evading basic issues such as censorship, other forms of community pressure, and the librarian's status in the community. Working concepts are essential to a profession, as more than one librarian observed, and inconsistencies in them may well be unavoidable, reflecting the attempt of the public library to be many things to many people. If so, they reason, greater effort in the training schools to locate and analyze these complexities might in itself contribute to a stronger sense of professional adequacy. "Professionalism," observed one graduate, "is an attitude, not just a set of skills or a bunch of jargon."

A similar attitude was taken toward the practical problems likely to be faced by the working librarian in his community. One respondent pointed out, for example, that many librarians consider "status" a concept proper to avoid. They often heard the word in their professional schools, but they did not examine the concept. Critics sympathetic to this viewpoint say that the schools discuss whether certain chores fall into professional or sub-professional levels of job activity, or the correct title for persons who check out books. But the more complicated problem of the librarian's status in his community, which (as the data of this study demonstrate) is intimately related to his freedom to function according to professional prescriptions rather than to public or bureaucratic proscription, is not squarely confronted.

These remarks about academia stem from the premise that, whatever their other attributes and function, libraries have primarily to do with books. Books have a bearing on human progress, and human progress involves processes which are primarily intellectual and educational. These critics say, in effect, that the training programs do not provide sufficient examination of basic premises, do not place the teaching of skills within the larger framework of goals.

Some respondents expressed the hope that the present study will help to enrich professional training in the light of the problems and uncertainties reported from the field. A few expressed fear lest the study report merely gather dust on the shelves. Further field research, particularly studies which shed light on the role of the library as seen by various segments of the community, was sometimes suggested as a means of feeding more substance into courses dealing with public library history and administration. In fact, the paucity of up-to-date documentary materials on the public library in the community was cited as one explanation for the lack of analytical instruction in the professional schools. It was also pointed out that a long-range basic research program might attract promising students to the library schools which sponsor them. More important, as one state leader observed, field research would provide much needed material for substantive arguments in the state, regional, and local professional organizations, especially discussions which would help them define the role of the library more clearly to their respective publics.

THE SELF AND THE INSTITUTION

Our respondents believe that the public holds both librarians and libraries in low repute. On the whole, they share the public's allegedly low opinion of the profession. They reject, however, and often fiercely, its negative or indifferent attitude toward the library as an institution.[6]

If one culls from the interviews the observations about what kinds of people librarians believe themselves to be, the picture is at best highly ambivalent. Out of about one hundred such comments, four negative traits were mentioned for every positive one. Much of what they dislike about themselves suggests that they apply the standards of the cult of the popular personality. But the positive qualities they stress come from a different frame of reference; they are proud of those attributes of mind and spirit which they believe run quite counter to the supposed components of popularity. However much they deprecate themselves, they do find some admirable qualities, and these qualities reflect the same values—respect for ideas, knowledge, and intellectual freedom—with which they imbue their institutions. The dilemma is that these values are too deeply ingrained to be shaken off simply because they are currently unpopular. Yet librarians do not feel strong enough as individuals or as professionals to assert them in the face of public disapproval or indifference. They are in conflict, and their distress is turned inward against themselves. By concentrating on their deficiencies in socially admired attributes and on self-improvement in this sphere, they avoid the silent war between their own values and those which they believe prevail in the community.

The negative traits for which librarians are most likely to indict themselves can be summarized in the adjectives "mousy" and "withdrawn." Self-consciousness about appearance is often acute. "Do I look like an airline stewardess?" asked a not at all mousy head librarian as she mused over the reasons why young people do not show more interest in the profession. Much of the sensitivity to the film *Storm Center* was the result of Bette Davis' appearance as a middle-aged woman, in sensible shoes, who wore only one hat in the whole picture. Some protest that dowdiness, though perhaps once a characteristic of librarians, is now no longer a just accusation, but their anxiety is betrayed by the frequency and often the vehemence of their protestations. The men, for their part, are often eager to create a new image of managerial aplomb.

Those librarians who had something good to say about themselves and their colleagues used such terms as "dedicated," "liberal," and

---

[6] A pilot study conducted as part of a graduate seminar given by the author at the School of Librarianship in Berkeley suggests that, while specific knowledge about the holdings and functioning of libraries and about the qualifications and activities of librarians is sparse even among well-educated patrons of the library, there exists, nevertheless, an impressive reservoir of goodwill toward both the institution and the profession.

"open-minded." By the same token, they criticized themselves for being too prone to compromise, too cautious or too evasive—for not speaking up about the values they most certainly hold. "Librarians," as one of them put it, "toe the mark too conspicuously."

By contrast, the conceptions librarians, particularly public librarians, hold of their work and of their institutions are almost entirely favorable. That it is wonderful work is a recurring theme; if people only knew how gratifying and diversified and important it is, they would have no recruitment problems. Aside from complaints about salary level, and they were remarkably few, public librarians made scarcely any derogatory comments about working conditions. Even school librarians, who do complain loudly, were not bitter about library work itself but about the requirements within the school system which prevent them from devoting enough time to it. Unlike the self-image, part of which is derived from the public stereotype, a high opinion of the institution is retained in spite of, sometimes in open defiance of, what is construed as a negative or indifferent public view. The executive of a public library, for example, is often aware, as one of them put it, of directing "a second-class city department." The salary of a head librarian may be only half that of the school superintendent in the same community, although the amount of general and specialized education required for the two positions may be identical. We live in a period when, as a young county librarian expressed it, "There may be some residual respect for the librarian, but it is only for his executive activities."

Most public librarians do not think in such detached terms, however. "We don't," as a county librarian remarked, "know how to look at ourselves from the outside." The result is an almost universal tendency to blame oneself or the profession for even those problems which most clearly have at least some social causation. For example, several women librarians (almost all of them heads of municipal or county libraries) believe that the future of the library rests with men. They did not say that women are discriminated against in professional or community situations, but that women are not as interested in, or as qualified for, participation in community life and in professional organizations as are men.

School librarians more often see themselves from "the outside" and adopt a social, sometimes almost sociological, point of view. They use social concepts in discussing their situation. They see a relationship between their self-image and professional problems on the one hand, and the structure of their institutions and the place of these institutions in the community on the other. They use the word bureaucracy, particularly those school librarians who work in large systems, with full awareness of its impact on their own attitudes and practices. As we have seen, they find the ever-thickening layers of curriculum coordinators and instructional supervisors incompatible with the primary functions of the library, if not with education itself. Many of them attribute their feelings of isolation to the weakening of human relationships which accompanies high faculty and student turnover and elaborate, formal methods of communication. But whether they attribute their difficulties to social or to psychological factors, school and public librarians alike feel unsure about what is expected of them —about what to expect of themselves. They have doubts about status and role which sometimes lead them to compromise their values, about which they have fewer doubts. Implicit—and often explicit— in their critiques of their organizations and training schools, is the hope that a reassessment and reassertion of these values by the profession will encourage the individual librarian to assert them in his own community.

The extent to which the restrictiveness and caution in California school and public libraries is indicative of situations in other states can only be conjectured. A review of incidents which have taken place on the East Coast and in the Midwest suggests that the episodes which have taken place in California are by no means unique. A few small studies which have been done elsewhere indicate that the internalization of indirect public pressures, one of the major findings of this study, may well be common to librarians and school administrators throughout the country. The attitudes and practices of librarians who took their professional training in other parts of the country suggest that it is also not too farfetched to assume that the stabilizing effect of professional training is by no means limited to California.

APPENDICES

APPENDIX A

TABLES

TABLE 1

COMMUNITIES AND INSTITUTIONS VISITED

Population class[1]	City	Growth rate[2]	Ethnic composition[3]	Community climate[4]	Cultural atmosphere[5]	Institutions[6]	Interviews[7]
100,000+	A	rapid	heterogeneous	restrictive	low	M + 3(b)	10
						C(nc) + 4(b)	7
	B	slow	homogeneous	permissive	high	6S[8] + Sq	8 + 8a
						MC + 3(b)	8
	C	rapid	heterogeneous	permissive	middle	4S + Sq	6 + 1a
						M	3
						C	4
						2S	2
	D	slow	homogeneous	permissive	middle	M + 1(b)	3
						C	4
						2S + Sq	2 + 2a
	E	rapid	heterogeneous	mixed	low	CM + 1(b)	6
						2S + Sq	2 + 2a
50,000-100,000	F	slow	homogeneous	mixed	middle	M	1
						2S + Sq	2 + 3a
	G	rapid	homogeneous	permissive	high	M	3
						S + Sq[9]	1 + 2a
	H	average	average	restrictive	middle	M + 1(b)	3
						C	1
						S	1
	I	average	average	restrictive	middle	M + 1(b)	7
						C + 1(b)	6
						S + Sq	2 + 1a
	J	slow	homogeneous	mixed	high	MC	4
						S + Sq	1 + 2a
25,000-49,999	K	rapid	heterogeneous	restrictive	low	M	1
						S + Sq	1 + 3a
	L	rapid	homogeneous	restrictive	middle	M	2
						3S	3
	M	average	average	restrictive	low	CM + 1(b)	5
						3S + Sq	4 + 4a
	N	rapid	homogeneous	mixed	low	M	2
						2S	2 + 3a
	O	rapid	homogeneous	permissive	middle	M	1
						C	3
						S + Sq	1 + 1a

					[6]	[7]
7,500-24,999						
P	rapid	homogeneous	mixed	middle	M / 3S	2 / 3 + 1a
Q	slow	homogeneous	mixed	high	M / S[7]	1 / 1 + .1a
R	average	heterogeneous	mixed	middle	M / C(nc) / S + Sq	2 / 1 / 1 + 2a
S	rapid	homogeneous	mixed	high	M / 2S	2 / 2 + 2a
T	slow	homogeneous	permissive	low	M / C(nc) / S	1 / 2 / 1
U	average	average	permissive	middle	M / S	2 / 1 + 2a
7,499-						
V	slow	homogeneous	permissive	middle	M / S	2 / 1 + 1a
W	average	homogeneous	permissive	high	M / C / S + Sq	1 / 1 / 1 + 2a
X	slow	average	mixed	low	M / S	1 / - / 1a
Y	slow	average	restrictive	low	M / S	2 / 1
Z	average	homogeneous	restrictive	middle	M / S	1 / 1 + 2a

[1]Based on latest authoritative population data available in January, 1957. Two cities were subsequently discovered to have moved into a higher population class. Cities were also distributed on a regional basis, within each population class:

[2]Relative to total urban growth rate in California, 1940-1950; rate for each city is for 1940 to date of latest authoritative population estimate available in January, 1957.

[3]Estimated. Census data do not include groups sociologically definable as "ethnic" (e.g., Mexican-born) which this report does consider as contributing to heterogeneity.

[4]Interviewer's estimate based on study of local newspaper, conversation with local residents, general observation, and the community's reputation.

[5]Interviewer's estimate.

[6]M: municipal; C: county; CM: county serving headquarters city; MC: municipal serving county by contract; S: school; Sq: school headquarters (and headquarters library if extant); (b): branch; (nc): non-circulating.

[7]Figure alone: librarians; a: administrators.

[8]Including 3 independent school districts within the metropolitan community.

[9]Part of a school system covering several communities.

TABLE 2

TYPES OF INSTITUTIONS VISITED

Type	Number
School systems[1]........................	29
Operating units......................	46
County library systems................	11
Operating units[2]	17
Municipal library systems	24
Operating units.....................	31

[1]Covering the basic sample of 26 communities plus 3 sub-communities in metropolitan Los Angeles.
[2]Including 3 non-circulating county headquarters.

TABLE 3

PERCENTAGE DISTRIBUTION OF RESPONDENTS BY AGE

(Age based on interviewers' estimates)

Respondents	Age					Number of respondents
	20-29	30-39	40-49	50-59	60 and over	
School librarians......	2	24	33	31	10	51
County librarians	3	17	27	33	20	40
Municipal librarians..	-	12	17	45	26	65
Total librarians[1]...	2	17	25	37	19	156
School administrators	2	2	42	50	4	48

[1]Mean age of public librarians is 51 years; mean age of school librarians is 47 years.

TABLE 4

PERCENTAGE DISTRIBUTION OF RESPONDENTS BY SEX

Respondents	Sex		Number of respondents
	Male	Female	
School librarians	14	86	51
County librarians	13	87	40
Municipal librarians	14	86	65
Total librarians	13	87	156
School administrators	98	2	48

TABLE 5

MARITAL STATUS OF RESPONDENTS
(Percentages)

Respondents	Marital status					Number of respondents
	Single	Married	Di-vorced	Wid-owed	Not ascer-tained	
School librarians	47	41	2	6	4	51
County librarians.....	35	48	5	5	7	40
Municipal librarians ..	31	49	3	12	5	65
Total librarians....	37	47	3	8	5	156
School administrators.	2	35	–	2	61	48

TABLE 6

DISTRIBUTION OF LIBRARIANS BY AMOUNT OF EDUCATION
AND PROFESSIONAL SCHOOLING
(Percentages)

Education and library schooling	School librarians	County librarians	Municipal librarians
College degree and librarianship degree or certificate[1]	77	67	52
College degree and incomplete librarianship schooling........	8	-	-
College degree or some college; no librarianship schooling	13	20	22
No college; some librarianship schooling[2]	2	5	9
No college; no librarianship schooling	-	8	17
Number of respondents	50	40	65

[1]Includes several who completed a six-month certification course prior to 1940 or in programs attached to major public libraries.
[2]Includes non-matriculating course attendance, incomplete degree work, one-year certifications, and certifications as in (1) above.

TABLE 7

DISTRIBUTION OF RESPONDENTS BY OCCUPATION
(Percentages)

Institution and occupation	Respondents
School systems (99 respondents)	
Superintendents	11
Superintendent-principals	2
Principals and vice-principals...............	25
Assistant superintendents and headquarters curriculum coördinators	10
Headquarters librarians	6
School librarians[1]	45
County library systems (40 respondents)	
County librarians (including acting librarians).	27
Other headquarters personnel	53
Branch personnel	20
Municipal library systems (65 respondents)	
City librarians (including acting librarians) ...	35
Other headquarters personnel	48
Regional and branch personnel..............	17

[1]Including two teacher-librarians. One school had no librarian.

TABLE 8

SOURCES OF BOOK-SELECTION INFORMATION MOST FREQUENTLY
USED BY LIBRARIANS

Source	Number of Institutions	Public libraries		School libraries	
		Librarians		Librarians	
		Use	"Rely"	Use	"Rely"
"Professionally authoritative"					
Library Journal	23	33	6	17	3
Wilson publications[1]...........	22	27	10	28	6
ALA Booklist.................	20	24	2	24	12
Horn Book	11	11	2	4	-
Book Review Digest	8	8	-	7	1
ALA special lists	4	4	2	14	3
Cumulative Book Index	3	3	-	2	-
Trade and commercial					
Kirkus' Service...............	25	40	11	1	-
Publishers' Weekly	16	25	1	-	-
Retail Bookseller	12	16	1	1	-
General sources					
New York Times Book Review..	23	29	1	10	-
Saturday Review	21	32	3	19	-
New York Herald Tribune					
Book Review..............	16	19	-	4	-
Local newspaper..............	6	6	1	-	-
Harper's	5	5	-	1	-
San Francisco Chronicle.......	5	6	1	4	-
Atlantic Monthly	4	4	1	1	-
New Yorker	4	4	-	1	-
Time	3	3	-	-	-
Other sources					
Publishers' or dealers' catalogs	10	10	-	4	-
Book clubs	9	9	1	7	-
Salesmen	8	9	3	-	-

Note: Figures used in text were computed from a full tabulation of every source mentioned (according to city size) from which this table is excerpted.

[1]Including, variously, the Bulletin and the Children's Catalog, Standard Catalog for High School Libraries, Fiction Catalog, and Standard Catalog for Public Libraries, and their supplements.

TABLE 9

OBJECTORS TO CONTROVERSIAL BOOKS IN PUBLIC AND SCHOOL LIBRARIES

(Percentages)

Objectors	School libraries	Public libraries
Librarian	42	65
Administrative personnel	23	-
Parent.............................	18	7
Teacher	8	2
Patron	6[1]	21
Other.............................	3	5
Number of respondents.............	95	132

Note: Data above is based upon cumulative figures for the three years preceding the study's field work.

[1]Students.

TABLE 10

GROUNDS FOR OBJECTIONS TO BOOKS IN PUBLIC AND SCHOOL LIBRARIES

(Percentages)

Grounds for objections	School libraries	Public libraries	Total, public and school libraries
Politics........................	29	16	22
Sex/obscenity	28	44	38
Profanity	10	12	11
Race, religion.................	7	8	8
"Controversial" or "unsuitable" .	11	7	8
Literary merit	7	8	7
Other	8	5	6
Number of respondents	95	132	227

TABLE 11

PRACTICES REGARDING CONTROVERSIAL MATERIAL,
BY COMMUNITY CLIMATE
(Percentages)

Practices[1]	Community climate		
	Restrictive	Mixed	Permissive
Habitually avoid	13	21	25[2]
Not a criterion	40	43	22
Number of respondents ...	62	38	55

[1]Excluding "sometimes" and "no opportunity"—see Table 14. Columns, therefore, do not total 100 per cent.

[2]Nearly all of these restrictive librarians living in permissive communities are accounted for by one city which has a centrally and firmly controlled school library system and a public library system directed by a restrictive, and for the most part non-professionally trained, headquarters staff.

TABLE 12

LIBRARIANS' EXPRESSED ATTITUDES TOWARD
CONTROVERSIAL MATERIAL
(Percentages)

Attitude[1]	School librarians	County librarians	Municipal librarians	Total
Freedom to read............	35	72	41	47
Weak, wavering or contradictory	35	23	39	33
Restrictive	30	5	20	20
Number of respondents	51	40	65	156

[1]Classification of expressed attitude was the product of an overall assessment of each respondent's opinions expressed throughout the interview. In almost every case, these attitudes were explicitly discussed. These discussions, in turn, were heavily supplemented by material from other portions of the interview—often, for example, arising out of explanations or justifications of specific behavior in problem situations, comments about the behavior of colleagues in such matters, or observations about the study itself. Thus, the two decisive classifications, "freedom-to-read" and "restrictive," represent clear overall tendencies. Two classifications were used in which neither of those seemed justified: "wavering or weak" —when the respondent seemed to express no really clear conviction or qualified it to the point of indistinguishability; and "highly contradictory"—when the respondent expressed attitudes at both extremes, equally forceably and seemingly unaware of their incompatibility.

TABLE 13

RELATIONSHIP BETWEEN PROFESSIONAL SCHOOLING AND ATTITUDE TOWARD CONTROVERSIAL MATERIAL
(Percentages)

	Freedom to read	Wavering or weak	Restrictive	Total number of respondents
Have professional schooling[2]	55	24	21	97[1]
Have no professional schooling	41	26	33	43[1]

[1]Excluding respondents with "contradictory" attitudes.
[2]College degree and librarianship degree or certificate.

TABLE 14

LIBRARIANS' PRACTICE IN REGARD TO CONTROVERSIAL MATERIAL
(Percentages)

Practices	School librarians	County librarians	Municipal librarians	Total
Habitually avoid............	29	5	17	18
Sometimes avoid[1]	29	45	49	41
Not a criterion............	38	37	29	34
No opportunity	4	13	5	7
Number of respondents	51	40	65	156

Note: Categories represent dominant behavioral tendencies synthesized from respondents' explanations of how they handle specific titles.

[1]If in spotlight or if avoidance can be justified for another reason.

TABLE 15

RELATIONSHIP BETWEEN ATTITUDE AND BEHAVIOR
REGARDING CONTROVERSIAL MATERIAL
(Percentages)

Behavior	Attitude[1]		
	Freedom to read	Wavering or weak	Restrictive
Habitually avoid	3	9	73
Sometimes avoid[2]	40	57	27
Controversiality not a criterion	57	34	–
Number of respondents ...	69	32	29

[1]Excluding respondents with contradictory attitudes.
[2]Avoid if book is in spotlight or if avoidance is compatible with a "legitimate" reason.

TABLE 16

LIBRARIANS' PRACTICES IN REGARD TO
CONTROVERSIAL MATERIAL,
BY CITY SIZE

Practices	Number	
	100,000 or more	Less than 25,000
School librarians		
Habitually avoid............	11	1
Not a criterion.............	3	9
Public librarians		
Habitually avoid............	5	3
Not a criterion.............	10	10

TABLE 17

LIBRARIANS' PRACTICES IN REGARD TO CONTROVERSIAL MATERIAL, BY ETHNIC COMPOSITION OF COMMUNITY

(Percentages)

Practices	Community ethnic composition[2]	
	Heterogeneous	Homogeneous
Habitually avoid	24	18
Sometimes avoid[1]	50	37
Not a criterion	26	45
Number of respondents	58	56

[1]Combines "avoid if in spotlight" and "avoid if justifiable on 'legitimate' grounds."

· [2]Because official census data, while distinguishing "racial" groups, do not distinguish ethnic elements (such as Mexicans) which must be taken into account in a sociological homogeneity-heterogeneity analysis, interviewers rated the communities on the basis of information available locally, rather than on explicit census findings. The three classifications, homogeneous, heterogeneous, and not-clearly-either, represent relative community profiles. (For example, while almost any city of more than 50,000 has a considerable number of ethnic or racial subgroups, one whose population has a rather small proportion of such persons relative to other cities in the sample would be classified as "homogeneous.")

TABLE 18

LIBRARIANS' PRACTICES REGARDING CONTROVERSIAL MATERIAL, BY PROFESSIONAL TRAINING

(Percentages)

Practices	Professional training	
	Yes	No
Habitually avoid	16	29
Sometimes avoid[1]...............	43	42
Not a criterion	41	29
Number of respondents	101	38

[1]Avoid controversial material if in spotlight or if avoidance can be justified on other grounds.

TABLE 19

PRACTICES REGARDING CONTROVERSIAL MATERIAL AMONG PROFESSIONALLY TRAINED SCHOOL AND PUBLIC LIBRARIANS
(Percentages)

Practices	Professionally trained librarians[1]	
	School	Public
Habitually avoid	30	7
Not a criterion	44 ·	33
Number of respondents	36	69

[1]Percentages do not total 100 per cent because other classes of practices do not appear.

TABLE 20

PRACTICES REGARDING CONTROVERSIAL MATERIAL, BY PLACE OF TRAINING
(Percentages)

Practices	Place of training[1]	
	California	Elsewhere
School librarians		
Habitually avoid	38	10
Not a criterion...............	38	60
Number of respondents........	(26)	(10)
Public librarians		
Habitually avoid..............	10	7
Not a criterion...............	34	43
Number of respondents........	(42)	(28)

[1]Columns do not total 100 per cent because other categories do not appear.

TABLE 21

PRACTICES IN REGARD TO CONTROVERSIAL MATERIAL, BY LENGTH OF EXPERIENCE IN LIBRARIANSHIP
(Percentages)

Practices	Years of experience		
	Less than 10	10-19	20 or more
Habitually avoid	15	16	24
Sometimes avoid[1]	29	45	52
Not a criterion	56	39	24
Number of respondents ...	39	44	58

[1]Combines "avoid if in spotlight" and "avoid if justifiable on 'legitimate' grounds."

TABLE 22

RELATION BETWEEN LENGTH OF EXPERIENCE IN LIBRARIANSHIP AND PROFESSIONAL TRAINING

Years of experience	Number of respondents[1]	Per cent with formal professional training
Fewer than 10	39	69
10-19	46	76
20-29	36	64
30 and more	28	68

[1]Excluding respondents for whom either experience or training was not ascertained.

TABLE 23

LIBRARIANS' PRACTICES REGARDING CONTROVERSIAL MATERIAL,
BY PARTICIPATION IN PROFESSIONAL ORGANIZATIONS
(Percentages)

Practices	Participation in professional organizations		
	Participating members	Join, no activity	No memberships
Habitually avoid	17	31	19
Sometimes avoid[1]	51	31	12
Not a criterion	32	38	69
Number of respondents	93	26	16

[1]Combines "avoid if in spotlight" and "avoid if justifiable on 'legitimate' grounds."

TABLE 24

PRACTICES IN REGARD TO CONTROVERSIAL MATERIAL,
BY READING OF PROFESSIONAL JOURNALS
(Percentages)

Practices	Reading in professional journals		
	Considerable[1]	Moderate[2]	Little or none[3]
Habitually avoid	13	30	24
Sometimes avoid[4]	50	35	34
Not a criterion	37	35	42
Number of respondents	59	34	29

[1]Read two or more journals regularly each month.
[2]Read one journal regularly or two irregularly.
[3]Rarely read professional journals.
[4]Combines "avoid if in spotlight" and "avoid if justifiable on 'legitimate' grounds."

TABLE 25

RESTRICTIONS ON CIRCULATION OF BOOKS IN THE COLLECTIONS
OF SCHOOL AND PUBLIC LIBRARIES
(Percentages)

Type of restriction	Circulating units applying restrictions		
	Total	School	Public[2]
Kept in office	33	41	27
Kept in reserve shelves or room........,	33	30	38
Removed from collection................	31	26	38
Kept under or behind circulation desk	27	17	38
Bought in a limited number of copies	15	2	29
Kept in locked cases....................	7	4	11
Other[1]	14	13	16
None	18	28	9
Number of units........................	91	46	45

[1]Labeling books with a symbol on the binding or on the circulation card to indicate that they are not to be checked out to particular classes of patrons (e.g., juveniles, or, in schools, below senior level) is among these; this is probably a more common practice than our data show—a shortcoming resulting from staff ignorance of such practices until well into the field work.

[2]Headquarters and branches separately, excluding non-circulating headquarters.

TABLE 26

GROUNDS FOR OBJECTIONS, BY CONSEQUENCES
(No time limit)

Grounds for objection	Not purchased, distribution restricted, or removed from collection
	Per cent of total restrictions
Politics................	19
Sex/obscenity	46
Profanity	10
Race, religion..........	9
"Controversial," "unsuitable"	8
Other.................	8
Number of respondents ..	186

TABLE 27

CONSEQUENCES BY ORIGIN OF OBJECTION
(Percentages)

Consequence of objection	Origin of objection	
	Outside the institution	Inside the institution
All libraries		
Restriction or removal of book.........	44	85
Book remains in circulation	56	15
Number of respondents	(70)	(158)
School libraries		
Restriction or removal of book.........	47	87
Book remains in circulation...........	53	13
Number of respondents..................	(19)	(78)
Public libraries		
Restriction or removal of book.........	71	84
Book remains in circulation...........	29	16
Number of respondents..................	(31)	(90)

TABLE 28

LENGTH OF EXPERIENCE IN LIBRARIANSHIP
(Percentages)

Years of experience	School librarians	County librarians	Municipal librarians
Less than 10	35	27	15
10-19	41	25	26
20-29	16	27	33
30 or more.............	8	21	26
Number of respondents ..	51	40	65

TABLE 29

MEMBERSHIP AND PARTICIPATION IN PROFESSIONAL LIBRARY ORGANIZATIONS
(Percentages)

Membership and participation	School librarians	County librarians	Municipal librarians
Active member[1]	56	75	67
Inactive member	28	10	17
Non-member..........	6	15	14
Not ascertained	10	–	2
Number of respondents	51	40	65

[1]"Active" indicates attendance at meetings or participation in committee or workshop activities (including, for school librarians, book review sessions), either currently or in the past year or two.

TABLE 30

LIBRARIANS' READING OF PROFESSIONAL JOURNALS
(Percentages)

Librarians	Reading of professional journals[1]				Number of respondents
	Consid-erable[2]	Moderate[3]	Little[4] or none	Not ascer-tained	
School	33	16	27	24	51
County..........	48	30	17	5	40
Municipal	43	25	18	14	65
All	40	24	22	14	156

[1]Material other than that directly involved in book selection.
[2]Reads two or more journals regularly each month.
[3]Reads one journal regularly or two or more irregularly.
[4]Rarely reads professional literature.

TABLE 31

COMMUNITY ACTIVITY OF SCHOOL AND PUBLIC LIBRARIANS
(Percentages)

Activity in community organizations	School librarians	County librarians	Municipal librarians
Active	22	33	31
Joins, but inactive	2	5	8
No memberships	33	29	21
Not ascertained	43	33	40
Number of respondents..	51	40	65

TABLE 32

SCHOOL LIBRARIANS' NON-LIBRARY DUTIES

Duties	Per cent who perform[1]
Handle textbooks	13
Supervise textbooks	44
Discipline	9
Study hall	11
Class in library science	36
Teach other classes	2
No non-library duties....................	20
Not ascertained	2
Number of respondents...................	45

Note: Headquarters librarians are excluded from this tabulation.

[1]Column does not total 100 per cent because of multiple entries.

TABLE 33

INFLUENCE OF SCHOOL AND PUBLIC LIBRARIANS AMONG OTHER LIBRARIANS

(Percentages)

Maximum range of influence in librarianship[1]	School librarians	County librarians	Municipal librarians
National................	4	5	2
State	4	13	11
Regional	16	15	15
Local	20	10	20
None	46	42	39
Not ascertained	10	15	13
Number of respondents...	51	40	65

[1]Based on current or recent leadership (holding office, active committee membership) in professional organizations and extent of active, informal professional contact.

TABLE 34

DISTRIBUTION OF LIBRARIANS' MEMBERSHIPS IN
PROFESSIONAL ORGANIZATIONS
(Percentages)

Organization	School librarians	County librarians	Municipal librarians
ALA	25	43	49
CLA	43	85	72
SLAC	65	3	-
No memberships	10	10	9
Not ascertained	12	3	6
Number of respondents...	51	40	65

Note: Columns do not total 100 per cent because of multiple memberships.

TABLE 35

PRACTICES IN REGARD TO CONTROVERSIAL MATERIAL,
BY PROFESSIONAL INFLUENCE
(Percentages)

| Practices | Extent of influence[1] | | |
	National, state, or regional	Local only[2]	None
Habitually avoid	6	27	24
Sometimes avoid[3]	50	46	35
Not a criterion	44	27	41
Number of respondents...	34	26	59

[1]Based on current or recent leadership (holding office, active committee membership) in professional organizations and extent of active, informal professional contacts.
[2]In non-metropolitan areas, this may include nearby communities.
[3]Combines "avoid if in spotlight" and "avoid if justifiable on 'legitimate' grounds."

INTERVIEW

SCHEDULES

Topical Outline for Interviews with School Librarians
(and School Administrators where Appropriate)

Introduction: Background of study; background of respondent (education, professional experience, professional affiliations, professional journals read, community affiliations).

I. BOOK SELECTION OBJECTIVES AND POLICY

A. Allocations

(1) How and by whom school library funds are appropriated and apportioned; how allocations in major categories (e.g., curriculum supplements, recreational reading) are arrived at; variations in allotments since pre-war period. (Also make note of any records kept, such as accessions lists, numbers of users, book use and turnover.)

(2) Use of library in curriculum (teachers and classes).

(3) Other uses of library (e.g., librarian as instructor on how to use the library; attention to non-curriculum interests of individual students).

(4) Objectives of book selection as described, for example, to new teachers or new classes of students.

B. Book selection policies

(1) Who participates in formulation (responsibilities of supervisor, committee of librarians, principal, librarian, teachers).

(2) Form of policy: verbal, written, or both; degree of specificity; use.

(3) History of written policy (if one exists): main purpose in drawing it up; who participated; extent written policies of other school libraries utilized; by whom reviewed and approved; action taken; extent of public knowledge of the policy (via posting in library, publication in newspaper, etc.).

(4) Changes in policies: pre-war, war period, post-war period.

(5) Differences in policies for different grade groups, if any.

(6) Principal's and librarian's appraisals of importance and value of written policies. Opinions as to why increasing numbers of schools seem to be adopting them.

II. BOOK SELECTION PROCEDURES

A. Persons involved: who on school staff suggests books; who coördinates suggestions; who actually orders them; who makes final review of order lists; comparative importance of student requests; approximate proportion of books requested by staff or students, but not ordered; which books or kinds of books; reasons; time spent.

If there is an order list issued from superintendent's office is it mandatory that no other books be ordered? If not, how are other requests handled? How many are accepted? How long does it take? Who prepares "central" list? Who does final reviewing? What proportion of books *not* on list are ordered annually?

B. Resources: amount of (formal or informal) staff discussion of particular books and of over-all allocations in any given order period; printed sources regularly reviewed; by whom; other sources such as formal or informal meetings or discussions with school librarians from other institutions. If a list is distributed from superintendent's office or by supervisor or libraries, does school librarian circulate this list; to whom?

III. PROCEDURES FOR HANDLING OBJECTIONS TO BOOKS

A. General description of procedures: written or unwritten; specific or general; substantive or procedural (or both).

B. When and by whom formulated; when and by whom approved; changes since pre-war period; plans for future changes.

C. Factors taken into account in formulation (e.g., to standardize staff procedures; to protect staff; to encourage support of board; to forestall public objections in general; to allay some particular objection).

D. Public awareness of procedures: Has procedure been publicized? Is it likely to be? Rationale for publicizing or not publicizing.

E. Are some books kept on "reserve" or "closed" shelves? Rationale? Which books? How does a student gain access to them? Other circulation restrictions.

F. Examples of public objections and action taken in each case.

(1) To policy or procedures

(2) To staff members

(3) To particular books or periodicals, categories or authors—include all kinds of objections, for example, "moral," religious, political, ethnic. (Note whether reviews are relied on in the case of a controversial book; which reviews, how used.)

(4) Pressures for additions, books or periodicals.

(5) Changes noted since pre-war period (e.g., in number and nature

of objections; characteristics and numbers of people who object; particular books or categories of books objected to).

(6) Relationships noted, if any, between objections to books and other objections pertaining to the school (e.g., social studies teaching, grading systems, etc.).

IV. ATTITUDES AND OPINIONS OF LIBRARIANS
(AND PRINCIPALS, IF CONCERNED)

A. General nature of own book selection philosophy: for example, leadership role of librarian; "good collection" versus "public demand"; definition of book selection as compared with book censorship. Bases for own philosophy; role of library school, professional organizations, colleagues—comparative importance of each.

B. Opinions of particular book selection policies and procedures.

(1) Efficacy of policies and procedures at own institution or in own school system.

(2) Impression of school book selection problems in other locales: for example, are there California communities which are notably free from such problems; are there communities or areas which have more severe problems? Why? Other parts of country?

(3) Opinion of actual and potential role of professional schools and organizations (local, county, state, and national) in clarifying and supporting book selection policies and procedures.

C. Discussion of: *Storm Center*; Murrow program; Marin County episode; "Mrs. X's" influence outside of Marin County; UNESCO controversies; School Library Bill of Rights; censorship bills—knowledge of first California bill, attitude toward; knowledge of and opinions about present bills pending in Sacramento.

D. Impression of local attitudes toward controversial books or authors. Which segments of public are concerned? Any change noted in numbers of persons so concerned? In types of material with which they are concerned?

E. How certain hypothetical objections would be handled: for instance, an influential person in the community complaining about
   (1) A book on religion
   (2) A pro-British book on American Revolution
   (3) A book with "too much sex"
   (4) A book on the United Nations
   (5) A book advocating desegregation
   (6) A book containing anti-Semitic or anti-Negro opinions

F. Own appraisal of certain categories of authors and books (e.g., trash, controversial books of various types, controversial authors).

G. Comparison of book selection problems of city, county, and school librarians. Impression of "public image" of public and school librarians (compare), and of public knowledge of their responsibilities and duties.

140 APPENDICES

H. Change in concept of librarian's role: Has this librarian's concept of the function of a librarian changed in course of his professional career? How? Does he believe that community expectations vis-à-vis libraries or librarians have changed? How?

I. Changes noted in own professional concerns (e.g., more worry about "public," about opinions of superiors or colleagues?).

J. Opinion as to whether there is a serious shortage of professional librarians and reasons therefor.

K. Librarian's duties and responsibilities in regard to textbooks: Does librarian have responsibility for ordering, inventory? Does she have assistance? How does she feel about this responsibility?

V. BACKGROUND DATA FOR COMMUNITIES AND INSTITUTIONS

VI. THE SCHOOL IN RELATION TO THE COMMUNITY

VII. BACKGROUND DATA FOR RESPONDENTS

Topical Outline for Interviews with Public Librarians

Introduction: Background of study; background of respondent (education, professional experience, professional affiliations, professional journals read, community affiliations).

I. BOOK SELECTION OBJECTIVES AND POLICY

A. Allocations

(1) How allocations in major categories (e.g., fiction, science, "do it yourself") are made. Changes noted, if any, since pre-war period. (Also make note of any records kept, such as accessions lists, numbers of patrons, book use and turnover.)

(2) How concept of "well-rounded library" is reconciled with public interest or demand. How public interest or demand are assessed.

(3) How general book selection objectives are described—to a new board member, for example.

B. Book selection policies

(1) Who participates in formulation (responsibilities of librarian, staff, trustees)?

(2) Form of policy: verbal, written, or both; degree of specificity; use.

(3) History of written policy (if one exists); main purpose in drawing it up; who participated; use of written policies of other libraries; by whom reviewed and approved; action taken; extent of public knowledge of the policy (via posting in library, publication in newspaper, etc.).

(4) Changes in written and unwritten policies—pre-war, war period, post-war period (e.g., from vague and unwritten to specific and in writing).

(5) Differences in policies for children's, youth, and adult collections.

(6) Librarian's appraisal of importance and value of written policies; opinion as to why increasing numbers of libraries seem to be adopting them.

II. BOOK SELECTION PROCEDURES

A. Persons involved: who on library staff suggests books; who coördinates suggestions; who actually orders them; who makes final review of order lists; differences between children's and adult division, if any; comparative importance of public requests; approximate proportion of books requested by staff or public but not ordered; which books or kinds of books, reasons; time spent.

B. Resources: amount of (formal or informal) staff discussion of particular books and of over-all allocations in any given order period; printed sources regularly reviewed; by whom; other sources such as formal or informal meetings or discussions with librarians from other institutions.

C. Gifts: how the problem of gift books is handled.

III. PROCEDURES FOR HANDLING OBJECTIONS TO BOOKS
(AND OTHER MATERIALS, IF APPLICABLE)

A. Description of procedures: written or unwritten; specific or general; substantive or procedural or both).

B. When and by whom formulated; when and by whom approved; changes since pre-war period; plans for future changes.

C. Factors taken into account in formulation (e.g., to standardize staff procedures; to protect staff; to encourage support of board; to forestall public objections in general; to allay some particular objection).

D. Public awareness of procedure: Has it been publicized? Is it likely to be? Rationale for publicizing or not publicizing.

E. Are books kept on "reserve" or "closed" shelves? Rationale? Are fewer copies of some books purchased than might conceivably be "needed"? What books? How does patron gain access to them? Other circulation restrictions.

F. Examples of public objections and action taken in each case.
    (1) To policy or procedures
    (2) To staff members
    (3) To particular books or periodicals (or records or films where applicable), categories or authors—include *all* kinds of objections, for example, "moral," religious, political, ethnic; note whether reviews are relied on in the case of a controversial book; which reviews, how used.
    (4) Pressures for additions, books or periodicals.
    (5) Changes noted since pre-war period (e.g., in number and nature of objections; characteristics and numbers of people who object; particular books or categories of books objected to).

IV. ATTITUDES AND OPINIONS OF LIBRARIANS

A. General nature of own book selection philosophy: for instance, leadership role of librarian; "good collection" versus "public demand"; definition of book selection versus censorship; bases for own philosophy; role of library school, professional organizations, journals, colleagues; comparative importance of each.

B. Opinions of particular book selection policies and procedures

    (1) Efficacy of policies and procedures at own institution.

    (2) Impression of book selection problems in other locales: for example, are there California communities or areas which have more severe problems? Why? Are there communities which are notably free of such problems? Why? Other parts of the country?

    (3) Opinion of actual and potential role of professional schools and organizations (local, county, state, and national) in clarifying book selection policies and procedures.

C. Discussion of: *Storm Center*; Murrow program; UNESCO controversies; Intellectual Freedom Kit (CLA); Library Bill of Rights; Marin County episode; "Mrs. X's" influence outside Marin County; censorship bills— knowledge of first California bill, attitude toward; knowledge of and opinions about present bills pending in Sacramento.

D. Impression of local attitudes toward controversial books or authors: Which segments of public are concerned? Any change noted in numbers of persons so concerned? In types of material with which they are concerned?

E. How certain hypothetical objections should be handled: for example, an influential person in the community complaining about

    (1) A book on religion

    (2) A pro-British book on American Revolution

    (3) A controversial medical or scientific book

    (4) A book with "too much sex"

    (5) A book on the United Nations

    (6) A book advocating desegregation

    (7) A book containing anti-Semitic or anti-Negro opinions

F. Own appraisal of certain categories of authors and books (e.g., trash, controversial books of various types, controversial authors).

G. Comparison of book selection problems of city, county, and school librarians. Impression of "public image" of public and school librarians (compare), and of public knowledge of their responsibilities and duties.

H. Change in concept of librarian's role: Has this librarian's concept of the function of a librarian changed in course of his professional career? How? Does he believe that community expectations vis-à-vis libraries or librarians have changed? How?

I. Changes noted in own professional concerns (e.g., more worry about "public," about opinions of superiors or colleagues?)

J. Opinion as to whether there is a serious shortage of professional librarians and reasons therefor.

       V. ORGANIZATIONAL, ADMINISTRATIVE, AND LEGAL STRUCTURE OF
         LIBRARY OR LIBRARY SYSTEM

       VI. THE LIBRARY IN RELATION TO THE COMMUNITY

       VII. BACKGROUND OF RESPONDENTS

CATEGORIES FOR

QUALITATIVE ANALYSIS

CATEGORIES FOR QUALITATIVE ANALYSIS

1. Administration; administrative problems (other than budget or personnel)
2. Assistance or support (to or from others, specific or "moral")
3. Attractions, advantages of librarianship
4. Authority in book selection

8. Balance (all references, any meaning; explicit or implicit)
9. Board's role (library, supervisors, education; specific or general)
10. Book content (specific topic or book, except complaint examples)
11. Book selection, general (complexity of; theory of; principles of; philosophy of)
12. Book Selection Study of the University of California
13. Budget; allocation
14. Bureaucracy; library structure; institutionalization
15. Book selection procedures, specific
16. Basic collection (explicit or implicit references)

18. Censorship, general (principle of; definition)
19. Censorship pressures, specific; any pressures or complaints re books
20. Change (any context, any meaning)
21. Character of clientele (except change)
22. Character of community (except change)
24. Civic groups in relation to library
25. Communication, channels of (in library or school; or library to/from other institutions)
26. Community, relation of library or librarian to
27. Competence in book selection.

28. Complaints in general, not coded elsewhere
29. Complaint procedure
30. Content of books, general
31. Content of education
32. Controversial material, general; definition
33. Coöperation (or absence of), any context
34. Cultural improvement
35. Civil service; tenure
36. Comparisons (any context, excluding change)

39. Evaluation (specific books)
40. Evaluation of books or library program in general; principles, importance of
41. Extremists, crackpots, minorities (general)

45. Formalization (except policy or complaint procedure)
46. Freedom to read, general
47. Friends of the Library

49. Gifts
50. Grand Jury

55. Ideology, general (not otherwise coded)
56. Image of librarians, self, other professionals
57. In-service training
58. Interests of readers
59. Intuition

65. Job attitudes
66. Job components

68. Leaders, leadership (specific or general)
69. Level of book content
70. Level of education content
71. Librarian's personal tastes, judgment, values in book selection
72. Library's role, function
73. Love or respect for books, ideas in books

77. Male-female contrasts
79. (Moral) commitment; dedication; emotional side of philosophy of librarianship
80. Murrow program

85. Negative aspects of librarianship
86. Non-professional personnel
87. Non-solicitation for professional memberships

94. Patriotism (general; aside from book content)
95. Personnel problems (other than shortage)
96. Philosophy of librarianship
97. Policy of book selection (any context, even if also listed elsewhere)
98. Politics
99. Professionalization, professionalism (except as below)
100. Professionalism's future; future of librarianship
101. Professional leadership
102. Professional organizations, own relation to
103. Professional organizations, role of
104. Protecting children
105. Protecting the collection; books disappear; mutilation
106. Protecting the system (board, librarians)
107. Psychology of reading
108. Public demands, need, requests (for books)
109. Public officials, other than board
110. Publicity, public relations, press relations
111. Programs, services for clientele

117. Removals (general or specific)
118. Restrictive practices (general or specific) in book selection or use of collection (except removals)
119. Rounded collection (any reference or implication)
120. Reading level (general)

124. Selection (general; principles of; definition)
125. Shortage of personnel
126. Smart
127. Sources, use or evaluation of, general or specific
128. Specialists, specialization (any context)
129. Standards (any sense, explicit or implied)
131. State supervision, law
132. Status of librarians, vis-à-vis community, other professions, other civil employees
133. Subversion, other than book content
134. *Storm Center*
135. State Library

138. Temper of the times; public interest
139. Taxpayer's rights
140. Textbook controversy
141. Time, use of
143. Training centers
144. Training, other than content or centers, importance of, problems of

149. UNESCO, UN, etc.

158. Young people